3 –

D0549028

THE YEARS BETWEEN

A dramatic view of the twenties

by Marvin Barrett

THE JAZZ AGE
THE YEARS BETWEEN

and thirties by Marvin Barrett

LITTLE, BROWN AND COMPANY, *Boston, Toronto*

THE YEARS

BETWEEN

COPYRIGHT © 1962 BY COLUMBIA BROADCASTING SYSTEM, INC.

ALL RIGHTS RESERVED. NO PART OF THIS BOOK MAY BE REPRODUCED IN ANY FORM WITHOUT PERMISSION IN WRITING FROM THE PUBLISHER, EXCEPT BY A REVIEWER WHO MAY QUOTE BRIEF PASSAGES IN A REVIEW TO BE PRINTED IN A MAGAZINE OR NEWSPAPER

LIBRARY OF CONGRESS CATALOG CARD NO. 62–9551

FIRST EDITION

The author wishes to thank the following for permission to quote from copyrighted and from uncopyrighted material:

New Directions for THE BERLIN STORIES by Christopher Isherwood. Copyright 1945 and 1954 by New Directions.

Cole Porter for an unpublished song.

G. P. Putnam's Sons for A KING'S STORY by H.R.H. Edward, Duke of Windsor. Copyright 1947, 1950, 1951 by H.R.H. Edward, Duke of Windsor.

Random House, Inc., for "Spain 1937" by W. H. Auden. Copyright 1940 by W. H. Auden. Reprinted from THE COLLECTED POETRY OF W. H. AUDEN. Also for "Two Armies" by Stephen Spender, from COLLECTED POEMS, 1928–1953. Copyright 1930, 1942, 1947, 1949, 1952, 1955, by Stephen Spender.

Viking Press for a quatrain from Dorothy Parker's "Not So Deep as a Well." Copyright 1936 by Dorothy Parker.

Published simultaneously in Canada
by Little, Brown & Company (Canada) Limited

PRINTED IN THE UNITED STATES OF AMERICA

This book is dedicated to my mother
ESTHER KRUIDENIER BARRETT
whose judgments were swayed by love,
but never by her own interest

FOREWORD

ALTHOUGH THIS BOOK is concerned with the two decades from 1918 to 1939, it doesn't pretend to be either all-inclusive or exhaustive. It was suggested by the admirable CBS News television series, *The Twentieth Century,* and much of it is based on the photographic and historical research brought together for individual programs in that series. The ultimate choice of subject matter, the mood and the manner of presentation, however, are mine.

When anyone lives through two decades, a certain amount of its history is bound to cling to him. When that person survives those two decades by two more, what has clung, and what is learned at one remove, form — if he has had the opportunity to recollect these in a reasonable amount of tranquillity — into patterns that for him, at least, have some significance.

These chapters represent memories refreshed and amplified; opinions reaffirmed or altered. They are subjective, in that many of the people in them and the events and places described are colored by my own direct experience. I tasted the dust that blew off the Great Plains and saw the skies dark with it. I saw the Okies drawn up beside the road, their radiators steaming, on the way to the promised land. The zoomorphic architecture of Southern California in the Twenties and Thirties and the rotating pantheon of Hollywood's stars were part of my early mythology. I stood in line to shake hands with the young Eleanor Roosevelt and got a message via postcard from Gertrude Stein at 27 Rue de Fleurus. The campaigning Hoover, and Lindbergh in triumph, passed on parade before my goggling eyes.

More than this: there was the world of the silver screen, vivider than life and more compelling; there were the newsreels and the radio — crystal set, battery and all electric — telling me what was happening or had happened. There were the headlines, the popular magazines, the books — dumped into a consciousness that, a fortnight later, could only partially recall the origins of what it had assimilated.

Never did a decade form itself so quickly or self-consciously into an "Age" as did the Roaring Twenties, the Golden Decade. Never was a decade so informed with a sense of mission, of imperativeness, of doom, as the Thirties. I have tried to light on subjects that epitomize or illuminate the spirit of these times.

Complete objectivity, or anything near it, I have not attempted. But then, complete objectivity has always seemed to me a function of sanctity — or total ignorance. Such objectivity as these essays have, and I do claim some, is the result of the corrective of research aimed at strengthening tenuous or correcting tenacious and erroneous earlier impressions.

As a nonpolitical journalist, an untrained armchair historian, I may be considered presumptuous to have undertaken such a book as the one that follows. But when one considers the vastness of the archives available to the research worker and their daily growth, the mountains of paper with raw and possibly relevant information upon it, the film, the wax, and now the tape that supplements it in ever-increasing amounts — then the single non-expert, non-specialist who dares to express an opinion somehow seems less presumptuous.

If, after these introductory words, this book cannot be looked at or read as proper history, or sociology, or journalism, then perhaps it can be approached as a new species of autobiography: one man's recollection and reconsideration of an experience and heritage common to many.

I should like to thank a number of people at the Columbia Broadcasting System who were most helpful in the development, research and clearance of vital material for this book: Burton Benjamin, Barbara Sapinsley, Murray Benson and Jules North.

CONTENTS

THE YEARS BETWEEN

INTRODUCTION

THE YEARS BETWEEN November 11, 1918, and August 23, 1939, are as clearly set off from those that precede and follow them as any two decades in the memory of man. Bracketed on one side by the abyss of the Great War, on the other by World War II, they form an island in time, detached, yet to our eyes preternaturally vivid. Their frame of violence and destruction exempts them, somehow, from conventional chronology — wrenches them out of line; makes courses, trends, movements difficult to plot across them. Even living them was an odd experience.

Undoubtedly, it was the shock of the war behind and the desperate pull of the war ahead that, within their span, seemed to make pleasures more intense and illusive, present accomplishment so imperative, aberrations of thought and behavior so commonplace. It was an interesting, colorful, bewildering, disagreeable time, when retreat into a cozy past was cut off, and ahead, the angle of the slope down which the world was sliding grew ever dizzier.

Strange, for The Years Between began on a note of high idealism, as high as the workaday world had ever heard. In a matter of weeks it had died away and been replaced by the counsels of disillusionment and irresponsibility.

The Years Between ended with a grim and unenthusiastic reacceptance of the responsibility that had been abandoned: the idealism of those few weeks at the end of 1918 and the beginning of 1919 would never return.

Standing at the threshold of these twenty crucial, fascinating years was a man who attracted to himself more of the world's hope and admiration than any living figure in history. At their end, it was the world's fear and hatred that were focused with unprecedented intensity on a single figure.

EVANGEL OF PEACE; PROPHET OF DOOM

THE BEGINNING of the Years Between was an end: the end of a war to end all wars; and, after a few weeks of fantastic optimism, the end of all the sudden hopes of plucking a just and permanent peace from Armageddon.

Woodrow Wilson, the twenty-eighth President of the United States, with his pince-nez, his lantern jaw, his manner of the stiff-necked Scotch dominie, by the sheer force of his extraordinary will tried to impose a magnificent ideal on an exhausted reality. His vision and his program promised something totally different for the future. Wilson's ultimate inability to instrument his ideals, the world's flirtation with and final rejection of them, cast a shadow straight across the Years Between. Wilson's tragedy was their tragedy: his failure, as implacably as a grenade with pin drawn, set their term.

"I have seen fools resist Providence before," said Wilson, the prophet, "and I have seen their destruction, as will come upon these again — utter destruction and contempt."

"That we shall prevail is as sure as that God reigns," said Wilson, the evangelist.

As so frequently before, the promise of the evangelist waited, the doom of the prophet arrived on schedule. But that was later.

THE ARMISTICE OF NOVEMBER 11, 1918, the day and hour of the beginning of the Years Between, represented a joyous release, a profound relief to the common citizens of the world. The realization that what had been a bloody reality for over four years was now a nightmare memory gave mankind pause. For a moment, it seemed possible for emotions that destroyed to reverse themselves and construct. The ideals which Wilson had insisted were America's reason for entering the war and which he reaffirmed again and again to the very moment of victory as the driving force behind its military success, illuminated, and, in some measure, sobered the celebrations of the victorious. At the same time they encouraged in the hearts of the defeated the expectation of something better than they otherwise could have hoped for.

It was to Wilson, their most recent enemy, not to the leaders of the Old World governments with whom they had begun their fight, that the Central Powers — Germany, Austria-Hungary, Bulgaria and Turkey — capitulated. It was his "Fourteen Points" that both sides, with varying degrees of reluctance and enthusiasm, sincerity and deceit, finally agreed must form the basis of the peace.

Independence of peoples, self-determination, no annexations, no indemnities, justice, right — a new order: free trade, freedom of the seas, freedom of mankind — these and a dozen other lofty goals seemed for the moment possible to a world that had just squandered ten million men and three hundred and thirty-eight billion dollars on a war which, until Wilson informed it, had little idea of where it might be heading — or where it had come from.

Woodrow Wilson, born in 1856 in the manse at Staunton, Virginia, the son of one Presbyterian clergyman and the descend-

ant back to the sixth generation of a half-dozen others, was a tardy reader and an undistinguished student at the outset of his scholastic career. This, however, didn't indicate an absence of high seriousness. "An old young man," the family's Negro man-servant described him, "who tried to explain the reason of things."

Wilson's mission as the instrument of justice and a new order was still unclear during his early employment as lawyer and teacher. As president of Princeton University and governor of New Jersey it became clearer. Wilson the academic leader went down before his enemies while fighting against social privilege. Wilson the governor somehow managed to cut himself free from the hampering integument of party politics to accomplish social good. As President of the United States (1913–1921) he brought that office to the height of its international prestige. No chief executive before or since has experienced such a widespread and uncritical respect.

Looking back nearly forty years, Herbert Hoover, an associate, admirer, and successor in office (although of a different party) saw "a man of staunch morals . . . more than just an idealist . . .

the personification of the heritage of idealism of the American people."

A detractor, critic and social historian Edmund Wilson, shortly after the President's death saw his namesake as a man "obdurate and ruthless, and excessively thin-skinned . . . sensitive to criticism from friends . . . suspicious and vindictive to his opponents . . . unable to deal with either except by overwhelming the one and overriding the other . . ."

To an outsider, the South African war correspondent William Bolitho, he was "the consecrated guardian of the principal hope of mass-humanity . . . self-appointed, like genius, but absolutely single-minded, authentic and sure . . . In Wilson, the whole of mankind breaks camp, sets out from home and wrestles with the universe and its gods."

Whatever the future might see in him, at the moment of the Armistice it was Woodrow Wilson who seemed most likely to determine that future's course. His estimate of the immediate past: "Everything for which America fought has been accomplished." His plan for the immediate future: to ignore precedent and go to Europe to help negotiate a fair and lasting peace, the first President ever to leave the country during his term of office.

"I am the servant of the nation. I can have no private thought or purpose of my own in performing such an errand," he told Congress. "The gallant men of our armed forces on land and sea have consciously fought for the ideals which they knew to be the ideals of their country. . . . It is now my duty to play my full part in making good what they offered their life's blood to obtain."

The words were noble and informed with hope; but the stiff faces of the "irreconcilable" Senators who heard them — William Borah, Henry Cabot Lodge, Albert Fall and Hiram Johnson, McCormick, Reed, Brandegee — carried a different message. Wilson was a glory seeker; Wilson played dirty politics (as a wartime president he had demanded but not obtained a Democratic congress); Wilson was an unrealistic visionary.

Nor did all resistance come from his foes in Congress. A large segment of his cabinet, and many of his sympathetic advisers, opposed his going. From Paris Frank Cobb wrote to the

President's principal aide, Colonel Edward House, of the perils awaiting:

> The moment President Wilson sits at the council table with these Prime Ministers and Foreign Secretaries he has lost all the power that comes from distance and detachment. Instead of remaining the great arbiter of human freedom he becomes merely a negotiator dealing with other negotiators. . . . Furthermore, personal contact between the President and these Prime Ministers and Foreign Secretaries, who are already jealous of his power and resentful of his leadership in Europe, must inevitably develop new friction and endless controversy. . . . The President, if he is to win this great battle for human freedom, must fight on his own ground and his own ground is Washington. Diplomatic Europe is all enemy soil for him.

The President, "obdurate and ruthless," or perhaps just overconfident of the justice of his cause and the reasonableness of mankind, ignored friends and foes alike.

"I realize the magnitude and difficulty of the duty I am undertaking," he said. "I go to give the best that is in me."

If America in the person of a hostile Congress had already begun to withdraw its support, however tentatively, from Wilson, the masses of Europe were of a different disposition. Hoover wrote:

> To them, no such man of moral and political power and no such an evangel of peace had appeared since Christ preached the Sermon on the Mount. Everywhere men believed that a new era had come to all mankind. It was the star of Bethlehem rising again.
>
> For the moment, Woodrow Wilson had reached the zenith of intellectual and spiritual leadership of the whole world, never hitherto known in history.

"No one has ever had such cheers; I, who heard them in the streets of Paris, can never forget them in my life. I saw Foch pass,

Clemenceau pass, Lloyd George, generals, returning troops, banners, but Wilson heard from his carriage something different, inhuman — or superhuman," said Bolitho.

Wherever he went — Paris, London, Rome — the roar of the approving, hope-intoxicated multitudes greeted him. Famine and pestilence and revolution overwhelmed Europe in the wake of war, but Wilson brought with him the cure.

It wasn't, however, the people roaring their approval that Wilson had to meet. It was Clemenceau, the French tiger with blood on his whiskers, and Lloyd George, the fighting Welshman who had been elected on a "Hang the Kaiser" platform; it was diplomatic Europe, "these Prime Ministers and Foreign Secretaries . . . already jealous of his power and resentful of his leadership."

On January 18, 1919, in the Salle d'Horloge at Quai d'Orsay, the Peace Conference opened. At first things went well. On January 25, the President addressed a plenary session of the delegates. "We are here to see, in short, that the very foundations of this war are swept away," he said, and proposed as his broom the League of Nations, which months before he had started to bind together straw by straw in a covenant for mankind's salvation.

On February 14, he presented the finished object, the covenant of the League, to the delegates:

"Many terrible things have come out of this war . . . but some very beautiful things have come out of it. Wrong has been defeated. . . . The miasma of distrust, of intrigue, is cleared away. Men are looking eye to eye and saying: 'We are brothers and have a common purpose. We did not realize it before, but now we do realize it, and this is our Covenant of fraternity and of friendship!' "

Whatever the parallax of their gaze, whatever the uncommonness of their unavowed purpose, the Prime Ministers and Foreign Secretaries agreed unanimously to write Wilson's covenant for a noble future into the treaty with Germany. At that moment the deaths of millions of men, women and children, the

"The roar of the multitudes"   *Paris, London, Rome*

destruction of a thousand cities and towns, were postponed. For a lightning flash, hope balanced possibility; then the scales trembled, the needle fell.

As the signatures of the deliverers of mankind dried, the miasmas of distrust and intrigue began to rise and thicken on both sides of the Atlantic.

At home, where Wilson returned in triumph to adjourn Congress, he was greeted by Henry Cabot Lodge and a cabal of thirty-seven other Senators determined to defeat a document which they claimed was "not only loose, ill-drawn, full of questions about which the signatories will be disputing within a twelvemonth, but . . . a breeder of misunderstandings if not of war."

There was no agreement, nor was there likely to be one. Fraternity and friendship, the welfare of all nations — America was starting to think — came second to the United States' own safe skin.

In Paris the miasma was suddenly even thicker. The Tiger's claws were bared; the Welshman's noose was searching for other victims. "They are evidently planning to take what they can get frankly as a matter of spoils, regardless of either the ethics or the practical aspect of the proceedings," said Wilson when he got reports of what the diplomatic mice were up to during his absence. "This is not going to be a game of grab. Everybody, we hope, is going to get justice. . . . Thank God I can still fight."

But the game of grab was far advanced, and it was for keeps. As Wilson clung desperately to his beloved League — the future's hope — Lloyd George, Clemenceau and Orlando of Italy, operating in the squalid and desperate present, scored point after point, grabbed, grabbed again and redealt. The Japanese got Shantung, the Sudeten Germans went to Czechoslovakia. One and a half million Austrians in the Tyrol were delivered up to Italy. Poland took a slice of Germany, France got a deal in the Saar. The man-

Return in triumph,
and then . . .

Wilson before Congress:

"Firm when pliancy might have saved the day"

dates over Germany's former colonies, which Wilson intended to be administered by small neutral nations, were taken over by his greedy allies. Military alliances, indemnities, returned from their unquiet and premature graves.

The dislike of avowed friends for the upstart preacher's son from the New World became increasingly apparent. "Clemenceau followed his movements like an old watchdog keeping an eye on a strange and unwelcome dog who has visited the farmyard and of whose intentions he is more than doubtful," observed Lloyd George; as for himself, he assumed the editorial "they": "They were impatient at having little sermonettes delivered to them full of rudimentary sentences about things which they had fought for years to vindicate when the President was proclaiming that he was too proud to fight for them."

"America, prodigiously enriched by the war," said Clemenceau, at a time when the United States was pouring millions of irretrievable dollars into the feeding and nursing of a quarter of Europe's population, "is presenting us with a tradesman's account that does more honour to her greed than to her self-respect."

Wilson called for the *George Washington* to stand in readiness for an honorable retreat. But he didn't go. As with the addicted gambler, the green table and the possibility of a last-minute reversal of fortune would hold him in thrall till the final stack of chips was lost. His stack was the League covenant.

"If I were a German, I think I should never sign it," said Wilson in a moment of lucidity when he looked over what he and his colleagues had wrought. But on June 28th, in the Hall of Mirrors at Versailles — the very room where Bismarck had proclaimed the German Reich half a century before — the Germans signed.

"Well, it is finished," Wilson remarked. "And, as no one is satisfied, it makes me hope that we have made a just peace; but it is all on the lap of the gods."

Lloyd George, Orlando,
Clemenceau and Wilson

Arm-in-arm with Clemenceau and George, he went out to see the ornamental waters play.

THE OPPONENTS

Harding and Lodge
Brandegee

The lap of the gods, for Wilson, was shallow and steep. The League of Nations covenant, the one thing the Prime Ministers had left him, his own Congress refused to accept without alteration. Firm, when pliancy might yet have saved the day, Wilson said with an irony whose bitterness escaped him, "Better a thousand times to go down fighting than to dip your colors to dishonorable compromise."

He took the issue to the people. In forty speeches in twenty-seven cities he cajoled, pleaded, threatened, demanded their support.

"The affairs of America are linked to the affairs of men everywhere . . ." he told them. "The hearts of men like Clemenceau and Lloyd George and Orlando beat with the people of the world. . . . See how the whole world turns with outstretched hands to this blessed country of ours, and says 'If you lead, we will follow.' God helping us, we will lead. . . . Dare we reject this treaty and break the heart of the world?"

The outstretched hands of Clemenceau, Lloyd George and Orlando were reaching at that moment into Germany, the Balkans, Africa, the Middle East. The heart of the world was calling us "Uncle Shylock."

Borah
Hiram Johnson

On September 25, 1919, in Pueblo, Colorado, gray-faced and afflicted with a painful tic, Wilson delivered the last speech of his career. That night he was stricken aboard his private railroad car and rushed, desperately ill, back to Washington.

"There will come sometime, in the vengeful providence of God," Wilson had told the unheeding burghers of Sioux City, Iowa, "another struggle in which not a few hundred thousand fine men from America will have to die, but as many millions as are necessary to accomplish the final freedom of the peoples of the world."

Harding

"You are betrayed," he had told the veterans of St. Louis.

Hiram Johnson
on the stump

The betrayed gave their answer by turning their backs on the President and on vengeful providence, and by voting for Warren Gamaliel Harding, a small-town back-slapper, handsome, hale

and hearty, without a sermonette to his name: against foreign entanglements, against self-sacrifice and unnecessary heroism; for poker, for bootleg liquor, ping-pong, golf, good times and "normalcy."

"In the existing League of Nations, world-governing with its superpowers, this Republic will have no part," Harding told Congress in April, 1921. "There can be no misinterpretation, and there will be no betrayal, of the deliberate expression of the American people in the recent election."

Betraying or betrayed, it took Woodrow Wilson over three years after his final irrevocable defeat to die. By then the Years Between were well advanced toward a destination he saw and dreaded, but could not help them avoid.

The stiffness of his neck and the strength of his convictions; his ruthlessness and his right-mindedness; his unwillingness to listen to advice and his high ideals, his virtues and his vices com-

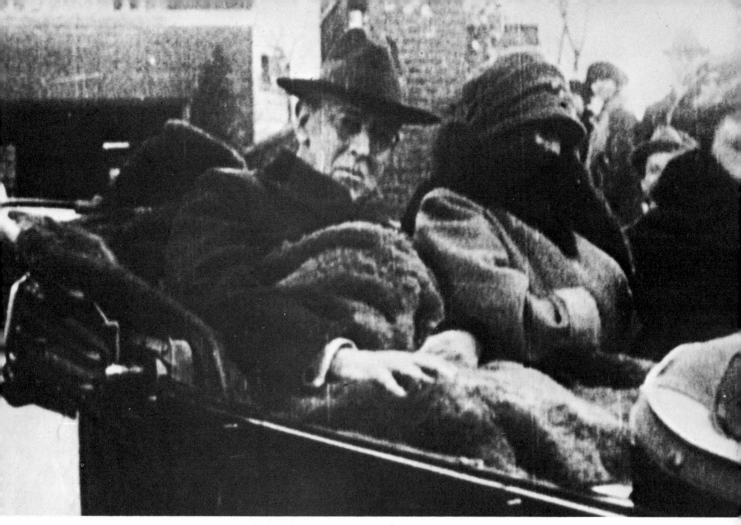

bined, had brought the world to the brink of the millennium. It teetered there momentarily and then drew back.

Whether it was a mistake in judgment, a failure in nerve, or the deadly inertia of a mankind so confirmed in wickedness that it couldn't bear the prospect of an earthly paradise, the retreat now became a rout.

The President's virtues and vices had once again joined forces, this time to destroy him, and what he stood for, utterly. First he had bargained with the mighty of the world when he should have held firm; then he had stiffened before the pettiness of his inferiors at home. In a man of less lofty principles, such actions would denote the bully, the opportunist, the poseur. In Wilson they implied a deadly vertigo. He had climbed so high; he was so inaccessible; so much was at stake.

With Wilson's fall, the main access to the future was cut off. The millions he would have saved began their fretful milling.

It was to last twenty years.

ACROSS THE RIVER
AND INTO THE HILLS

WITH THE DEMANDS of idealism swept under the green baize, with self-sacrifice and heroism abandoned at the moment when they could have been most spectacularly put to use, the Years Between addressed themselves to the pleasures of the body and the imagination.

Of these heady realms there were twin capitals.

One was Paris: the City of Light, the resort of the privileged by virtue of birth, income, talent, or their own resourcefulness. To the disappointed and the apprehensive, it offered the solace of gray stone and wide boulevards, incomparable food and drink, compliant flesh, and the companionship of the creative and untrammeled.

The other, for those who couldn't wangle steamship passage or were indifferent to such comforts, was Hollywood: the City of Flickering Shadows. Here, as close as your local cinema palace — passage twenty-five cents plus trolley fare — was Xanadu, a portable city of dreams, set up like Potemkin's villages at every crossroads, awaiting, not an Empress and her court, but Everyman, Everywoman, Everychild. Pagan revels, luxury unheard of, faces of intolerable beauty and irresistible manly appeal, sin and sentiment and slapstick — all available for instant participation, at one safe remove.

The City of Light; the City of Flickering Shadows — Wilson, the man of action and ideals, would have found his satisfaction in neither. But for those subjected to the eddies and crosscurrents of Babbittry and Boom, of rampant materialism and craven procrastination, they seemed legitimate havens. For a few brief years they remained Eldorados for the morally dispossessed.

The Paris that the interbellum elite flocked to was the product of two thousand years of pain and glory, the masterwork of a resourceful race and its distinguished guests. Its atmosphere, traditions, way of life, like its architecture, were worn and burnished to a rich glow by the slow, arduous processes of history.

Paris in the Twenties — flossy and jazzy as it was for some, grim and disillusioning as it must have been for others — contained the memories and monuments of the Paris of Lautrec, of *La Vie de Bohême*, of eighteen Louis', of Voltaire, Victor Hugo, and Villon. To look at, Paris was incomparably beautiful: Notre Dame and Sainte-Chapelle, the Place Vendôme, the Place de la Concorde, the Place des Vosges, the Étoile, the Île de la Cité, Montmartre . . . the Tuileries, the Luxembourg, the Bois de Boulogne . . . To live in, it offered endless delights and stimuli.

On the Right Bank, the girls in their bobs and their sheaths from Coco Chanel, the men in their doublebreasted tuxedos from across the Channel, might move down the Champs Élysées enveloped in their own personalized moral vacuum, but they left behind them the Arc de Triomphe, and before them, through an arching alleyway of chestnuts, was the Louvre.

If a large group of those who visited Paris in the Years Between possessed, as Scott Fitzgerald uncharitably contended, "the

IN PARIS:

La Belle Josephine . . .

human value of Pekinese, bivalves, cretins, goats," they were animals invading splendor — dining in the precincts where Cardinal Richelieu had once dined, lodging, if they stayed at the Ritz or the Crillon (and who on the Right Bank stayed anywhere else?) in the dwelling places of the grand of a grander era. Looking out their chamber windows on the morning after, they faced, however blearily, Napoleon's triumph bodied forth in a column cast from the melted cannon of Austerlitz, or the pavements upon which the tumbrel bearing Marie Antoinette stopped for the final time.

On the Left Bank, the youngsters in their beards and berets, amateur *apaches*, bargain-basement Bohemians, acted out their comedies and tragedies in an arena honored by the former presence of Abelard and Baudelaire, Rodin and Corot and Oscar Wilde.

and la Rive Gauche

Nor was it all frivolity and self-delusion.

"It was extraordinary how so many of us — without money — with a sense of pleasure and excitement had gone to Paris," said Janet Flanner, Genêt of the *New Yorker,* who came fresh from Indiana to rub shoulders with her fellow expatriates along the banks of the Seine. "We went willingly and gladly and lived grandly — on little money. Wine was so cheap — you know — that it seemed as if you drank it for nothing. Excellent food in small bistros. A wonderful sense of excitement in the city — so full of writing and literature. . . . That's what called men like Hemingway — that's what called a woman like Gertrude Stein — that must have been, even, what called Picasso."

Miss Flanner echoed the words of other visitors to Paris. "The nerve center of the arts," said Stella Bowen. "Here is life more noble than anything machinery has yet achieved," said Sherwood Anderson. "As an artist a man has no home in Europe save Paris," Nietzsche had written once with categorical firmness. It seemed that it had always been so. But, more than ever before, the fastidious of the world were looking now to Paris for inspiration and for distraction.

Paris was rock; Hollywood, spun sugar.

The physical Hollywood rose overnight from a cluster of citrus groves midway between the unrecognizably distended *Pueblo de Nuestra Señora, la Reina de Los Angeles de Porciuncula* and the vast impersonal salt bath of the Pacific. It had the look of an aerodrome whose runways some vast tidal wave had littered with architectural debris. Its most imposing edifices were all front and no back, prefabricated and easily dismantled: the fantastic escarpments of scaffolding and simulated stone built by David Wark Griffith to beetle over the Feast of Belshazzar in his film spectacle *Intolerance;* the Antioch coliseum built by Irving Thalberg, to house the ten thousand extras in bedsheets and the cowboy charioteers of the first *Ben Hur.*

The homes of Hollywood, on every income level, were "gorgeous" and phantasmagoric. Mexican ranch houses, Samoan huts, Mediterranean villas, Egyptian, Aztec and Japanese temples,

Swiss chalets, Tudor cottages, Spanish haciendas, Trianons, great and small.

The eating places of Hollywood were not accommodated in a cardinal's palace but in papier-mâché derbies, mammoth oranges, colossal bulldogs, stupendous ice-cream cones balanced miraculously right-side-up against a landscape of straggling pepper trees, dusty palms, shaggy eucalyptus and mauve-pink mountains. On such premises, mushroomburgers and jumbo avocado frappes, soybean steaks and carrot juice were legitimate food and drink.

But Hollywood, a city neither to live in nor to visit, had still more claim than Paris to the title "Capital of the World." This was the spiritual home of the Years Between, the non-Jerusalem, the anti-Rome. To a generation without a future, cut off from the faiths of the past, Hollywood unreality was realer than what they saw around them. It had to be. In its mass-produced dreams its gods and goddesses, thirty feet from chin to brow, bodied forth the fantasies and delusions of mankind without direction.

To anyone who doubted, it was only necessary to track the deities on an international progress; *Dougla* and *La Fiancée du Monde*, Lampo and Maria, Charlot, Chap, *Lui*. Meester Veelson with his message of salvation had briefly disrupted traffic in a trio of European capitals; these paragons peddling *dolce far niente* immobilized London, Paris, and Rome — plus Oslo, Stockholm, Copenhagen, Amsterdam, Warsaw, Moscow, Tokyo. Name it and they could have it, on its knees.

For Hollywood's specialty was glamour, the illusion of beauty and majesty, endlessly and cheaply reproduced. Paris by hus-

THE GODS AND GODDESSES OF ANTI-ROME:
Valentino and Mae Murray
Pickford, Fairbanks and friends
Valentino and Nazimova in CAMILLE
Mary Pickford at home

banding her resources and cultivating them had produced the real thing.

With filaments of celluloid Hollywood entangled the whole world in her myth. But, as with most myths, this one depended upon distance to endow it with conviction. Pilgrims to Paris found stone and stained glass they could stare at and penetrate, street cafés to loll in, a cake of custom to nourish them. Those who came to Hollywood were kept from paradise, according to one visitor, Lady Diana Cooper, by the walls and barbed wire of studios "like a dockyard or lunatic asylum with 'abandon hope' gates only opened for the bosses and holders of red-tape permits that need to be signed repeatedly."

In the hills above, where the persistent searched for their ideal on rubberneck tours of "movie stars' homes"; at the papier-mâché derby (if they could get in); in front of theaters pretending to be Chinese pagodas or Egyptian tombs where premieres were held (if they could elbow their way to the first rank): here they might get a glimpse of a god or goddess made flesh. But even those natives who walked the fabled streets, day after day, seldom pieced together enough of the reality to shatter the illusion re-established each night on the world's fifty thousand silver screens.

The capitals of the Years Between had concierges, gatekeepers who screened arrivals and doubled as mistresses of ceremonies.

In Paris on the Left Bank, it was Gertrude Stein. Holding court at 27 Rue de Fleurus in Montparnasse, she stretched on a divan below her priceless bargain Cézannes and Picassos, provided her guests with cucumber sandwiches, cookies, China tea and dashing conversation. With people as well as pictures Miss Stein dealt in future more than present eminence. Her judgments were sibylline and often, as with oracles, subject to more than one interpretation.

Into her ken chugged the young Ernest Hemingway from Oak Park, Illinois. "Hemingway was yellow," she pontificated later, "just like the flat-boat men on the Mississippi River as described by Mark Twain . . . extraordinarily good-looking . . . and ninety percent Rotarian." It didn't seem a particularly flattering commentary, but nevertheless Miss Stein stood godparent to Hemingway's son, midwife to his celebrated style.

Sherwood Anderson, in flight from the brutalizing drabness of "Winesburg, Ohio" and a properous paint business, "moved and pleased" Miss Stein as "she has very rarely been." This he did by finding her writing delightful when most of the world, even her friends, found it simply unintelligible. She repaid the compliment with a handmade "Valentine to Sherwood Anderson." "Very fine is my valentine. Very fine and very mine," it went, and although it continued for some time, it stayed very much in the same place.

Glenway Wescott, fresh, or nearly fresh, from Wisconsin (he had stopped somewhere along the way to adjust his manner of speech) "impressed us greatly by his english accent" Miss Stein reported through her amanuensis, Alice B. Toklas, a small lady with a mustache, who also made the cookies and sandwiches, and presided slyly at the teapot. "He has a certain syrup but it does not pour."

There was Ezra Pound, in velvet jacket and trilby, out of Idaho by way of London. "Gertrude Stein liked him but did not find him amusing. She said he was a village explainer, excellent if you were a village, but if you were not, not." Pound was almost as grudging in his praise of Paris. "Fools abound but are less in one's way here. . . . Only certain lands will produce copper. . . . Must go where the stuff is, no getting figs of thistle bushes."

T. S. Eliot, whose poem *The Waste Land* became the theme song of despair in a feckless era, arrived at 27 Rue de Fleurus shielded by an English peeress. Eliot of St. Louis, Missouri, as British as chilblains, and Miss Stein of Baltimore, Maryland, as American as a dollar bill, "had a solemn conversation, mostly about split infinitives and other grammatical solecisms and why Gertrude Stein used them."

There was Elliot Paul, "a new englander, but a saracen"; Louis Bromfield, "as american as a doughboy, but not as sol-

Alice B. and Gertrude . . . cucumber sandwiches and dashing conversation

Picasso

Joyce

Davidson and Stein

Sylvia Beach at
Shakespeare and Co.

Art outdoors

Eliot

Fitzgerald and family

emn"; Jo Davidson, who did Gertrude's portrait in bronze; Man Ray, who took her photograph; Virgil Thomson, who did the music for her *Four Saints in Three Acts;* Jean Cocteau, who communicated by letter from the Right Bank, where he ran a club, Le Boeuf-sur-le-Toit, which answered the most sophisticated entertainment requirements of a select group of the rich, talented, snobbish, bored and depraved.

There were also George Antheil, whose *Ballet Mécanique,* scored for anvils, motor horns, sixteen player pianos, and airplane propellers, blew the toupees off front-row customers and caused a riot among the outraged at its premiere at the fashionable Théâtre des Champs Élysées; Tristan Tzara, the leader of Dada, the most scandalous art movement of all time, which ridiculed all art, staged exhibitions in urinals, held inaudible poetry readings, made movies by sprinkling salt and pepper, pins and thumbtacks on strips of raw film. As frequently as Dada manifested itself, that frequently did the gendarmes have to be called to subdue incensed Parisians. "Tzara when he came to the house," Alice reported the disappointment of the Stein ménage, "sat beside me at the tea table and talked to me like a pleasant and not very exciting cousin."

Picasso, Gertrude's "dearest friend," quarreled and made up, quarreled and made up again.

F. Scott Fitzgerald arrived. The Jazz Age's Golden Boy and the Baltimore sibyl got on exceedingly well. "Fitzgerald will be read when many of his well-known contemporaries are forgotten," said Gertrude, although it was common knowledge that Fitzgerald drank too much, spent his substance on reckless Riviera living, and had been for his painful habits compared by Edna St. Vincent Millay to "a stupid old woman with whom someone has left a diamond."

The Sitwells, nobby and eccentric as they come, came: Edith

Edith Sitwell at home (Photo by Beaton)

with her magnificent nose, "the most distinguished . . . I have ever seen on any human being," and Osbert with his manner "like an uncle of a king."

And bookseller Sylvia Beach: "Her little place was in a little street near the École de Médicine. . . . It was not then much frequented by americans. . . . There were a few stray irish poets." One of these strays was James Joyce, whose masterwork *Ulysses* would appear under the humble imprint of "Shakespeare and Company," the name of Miss Beach's poky and friendly bookstore.

Ford Madox Ford, novelist and briefly editor of the *transatlantic review,* was a friend despite the fact that his parties rivaled Miss Stein's in drawing power among aspiring artists and writers — offering, as they did, dancing and liquor as well at literary counsel. In Paris between the wars there was room for both.

A plague on both your houses sounded from across the sea. "Ford and Gertrude Stein," scolded Van Wyck Brooks, "playing into the hands of Joyce, Eliot and Pound, provided a diet of nightingales' tongues for boys who knew nothing of beef and potatoes; and the maternal Miss Stein and the fatherly Ford appealed to their filial instincts also—which made the authority of these writers all the more compelling . . . victims of their own personalities . . . floating in a void . . . mystagogues . . . coterie writers . . . infantile." On and on he scolded, and on and on the talented youngsters came.

For most of the twenty Years Between, Miss Stein sat directing this traffic, filled with the flashing lights of genius, in and out of her parlor. She wasn't dazzled. A woman born before her time, she saw it quicken its pace under the lash of the Great War and fall in beside her. A literary prophet without honor in her own country, she shrewdly chose the place and time in which to set up her shrine, and was more than ready to collect the flattering attentions of her fellow countrymen, when, as if by instinct or prearrangement, they began to arrive.

Looking over her younger guests, Miss Stein pronounced them "all a lost generation." They were lost in order to write *The Sun Also Rises* and *The Great Gatsby; Three Soldiers* and *The*

Enormous Room; The Bridge and *The Grandmothers,* and a dozen others.

Miss Stein's bailiwick was the Left Bank — the quarter of Paris that, for a few brief years, gave its casual and tonic hospitality to the talented survivors of one disaster before the next descended. It was the Paris of the "little" magazines with the odd, emphatic names — *Broom, Fugitive, Secession, transition, Gargoyle;* and of the "little" press — Obelisk, Black Sun, Three Mountains, Contact — friendlier to the unknown experimenter than the sure-fire familiar. It was the Paris of the café noisy with earnest and outlandish talk — the Select, the Dôme, the Rotonde, the Closerie-des-Lilas, the Flore, the Deux Magots.

There was another Paris, where another massive American spinster was self-appointed mistress of ceremonies — Elsa Maxwell, "Queen of Paris" and creator of the newly founded "international set." Wrote a charter member, Cole Porter:

I'M DINING WITH ELSA, WITH ELSA SUPREME.
   I LONG TO MEET PRINCESSES
DRESSED IN COCO CHANEL DRESSES
   GOING WILD OVER STRAWBERRIES AND CREAM.
I'VE GOT BROMO-SELTZER
   TO TAKE WHEN DINNER ENDS
FOR I'M DINING WITH ELSA AND HER 99
   MOST INTIMATE FRIENDS.

According to one authority, the international set set in when declining European nobility met American money on the rise. Elsa was there at the moment of collision. It was even hinted that, for a lark, she switched them onto the same gold-plated tracks. At any rate, in the ensuing confusion the menace from Keokuk got a comfy Pullman berth for herself and coach space for a passel of her buddies.

If the Left Bank was concerned with art for art's sake, Elsa and her "99 most intimate friends" were after fun for fun's sake. For Elsa, even the geniuses scaled themselves down to party size. Diaghilev's Russian ballet performed at galas at the Ritz. Kreisler,

Horowitz and Gershwin came on as after-lunch or -dinner entertainment. Marilyn Miller did extemporaneous dances during cocktails. Bea Lillie, Noel Coward, Gertrude Lawrence sang for supper.

There were the world's first "Come as you are" parties, "Come as your opposite" parties, "Come as your secret passion or your bête noire" parties; treasure hunts with impossibly sophisticated clues; scavenger hunts with lists to stump Jason himself — a slipper from Mistinguett, a black swan from the lake in the Bois du Boulogne, a handkerchief from the breast pocket of Paris's most elegant boulevardier. In Bentleys and Bugattis, the gay hunters tore through every *arrondissement* — and more often than not ended up in the local gendarmerie.

Sooner or later everyone who was anyone anywhere joined the perpetual celebration. Millionaires and heiresses, barons, counts, marquises, dukes, grand dukes, Serene and Royal High-

EVERYONE FROM ANYWHERE WAS THERE

Marilyn Miller danced at cocktails . . .

nesses, the Prince of Wales, Queen Marie, King Gustav V of Sweden, the Aga Khan.

It was difficult to determine who was entertaining, who being entertained; who gawking at whom: Josephine Baker, the daughter of a St. Louis washerwoman and star of the Folies Bergères, or the dukes' daughters she danced among; Maurice Chevalier, or Baron Maurice de Rothschild; the Dolly Sisters, Hungarian peasant girls dressed like princesses, or the seedy Middle European noblemen who sought the fortunes the Sisters had already found; the King and Queen of Spain, or Cole Porter, who played the piano for them and had sixteen dressing gowns, nine cigarette cases and in his mansion on the Rue Monsieur a drawing room that *Vanity Fair* said was "done entirely in platinum."

Vanity Fair and *Vogue* were the Bibles of this effervescent world; and France's greatest woman writer, Colette, was doing

Michael Farmer, Noel Coward, Gloria Swanson,
Clifton Webb and Gertrude Lawrence
at the Café de Paris

Mistinguett at the Folies

their fashion copy. Staring at the latest slab-sided creations of Chanel, Lanvin, Poiret and Patou, this longtime champion of femininity occasionally balked. "Even the butcher knows that you must put lace paper round a leg of mutton." She now and then yearned openly for the return of "smooth curves, the arrogant bosom and the luscious hip"; observed apprehensively the arrival of the latest shipment of American mannequins: "This squadron of archangels, in its chaste flight, unhindered by any flesh, will draw fashion towards a line always more and more slender, towards clothes still more simplified."

Beaded, fringed, sequined, spangled, shot with gold and silver, the waistless, bustless, hipless parallelogram persisted.

Still to be seen, in top hat and otter-lined greatcoat in the corner of the hall at the Ritz at midnight, was another great writer, Marcel Proust, "a tottering young man of fifty." Once a patent-leather dandy who would borrow a golden louis from the Ritz's formidable porter and flip it back to him as a tip, now his cuffs and collars were frayed, his white gloves dirty, his hair uncut and his mustache seedy. But his was to be the final word on the confusion that he had observed with heavy-lidded eyes overtaking the elegantly ordered, neatly stratified society of before the war.

Into the hullabaloo of chic and intellect that overtook and buried Proust, a young god descended in a silver monoplane. Charles Augustus Lindbergh, all alone all the way from New York, arrived at Le Bourget airdrome — and Paris went wild. Heroism, clean living, for a moment took on glamour in the person of this lanky, curly-headed youth.

"This young man from out of the West brings you better than anything else the spirit of America," said Ambassadar Myron Herrick. "His exploit shows you that the heart of the United States beats for France. It was needed at this moment that

Elsa and Bea Lillie en travestie

the love of these two great peoples should manifest itself, and it is this young boy who has brought that about."

The gold medal of the Municipality of Paris was given him, and after a few days Lindbergh returned the compliment by circling the Eiffel Tower and dropping "a note of good-by and thanks to Paris" onto the stones of the Place de la Concorde as, once again alone, he flew to the north.

It was 1927, and others were moving southward.

"They all just slip down through Europe like nails in a sack until they stick out of it a little into the Mediterranean Sea," wrote Fitzgerald, playing both banks of the Seine against the Côte d'Azur. Antibes, the fabled Hôtel du Cap and Eden Roc: "just a real place to rough it and escape from all the world" — along with Rudolph Valentino, Mistinguett, Rex Ingram, John Dos Passos, Archibald MacLeish, E. Phillips Oppenheim, Floyd Dell, Max Eastman, ex-premier Orlando, Étienne de Beaumont and many, many more. "Pretty much of anything went at Antibes . . ."

"By 1928, Paris had grown suffocating. . . ."

"By 1929, at the most gorgeous paradise for swimmers on the Mediterranean no one swam any more, save for a short hangover dip at noon . . . the Americans were content to discuss each other in the bar."

Scott and Zelda had almost had it.

Nothing gay and amusing ever lasted very long [Ford Madox Ford's biographer observed]. Over and over again cafés acquired a vogue from the fact that well-known artists and writers were in the habit of frequenting them. The tourists would arrive in hordes, to listen and gape, and when they did so the artists fled, carrying their elusive "Bohemia" with them.

Already rendered self-conscious by the knowledge that they were acting out a living legend, the creative and gay of Paris were further subdued by the crash of the bull market and its dreary aftermath. The festivities of those idle rich who remained were dampened by the proximity of poverty — the sudden realization, no longer deferrable, that the mistakes of Versailles were bound, one by one, to come home to roost. The art-for-art's-sakers had second thoughts. Art could be propaganda. Art could be a living. For these pursuits, Moscow and Hollywood offered a more congenial climate.

"Better the breadline at home than starvation in a Paris garret," said one defector.

"By the Thirties, the Left Bank had changed. . . . Many of my friends had gone home," reported Sylvia Beach. "I missed them, and I missed the fun of discovery and the little reviews and the little publishing houses. It had been pleasanter emerging from a war than going toward another one."

Paris in the Twenties lived for itself, for art, for a good time. Hollywood, despite its air of fantasy and fun, lived determinedly for others. Dealing in cloud castles and will-o'-the-wisps, it was earth-bound, sober, practical, forced by its addiction to success to put other people's pleasures before its own. Refusal to obey this law could lead to professional death.

"In Movieland," a contemporary reporter, Carl Hovey, explained, "existence has the advantage of becoming intensely simple, and utter concentration is readily arrived at. In this great plant the electric tension of studio activity vibrates uninterruptedly in the blood of the workers. At night the shadowy peace of the desert mountains bestows complete recuperation for another day, when the battle begins fiercer than ever before. And so on, until all account of time is lost (except shooting schedules), when every outside interest has slipped into second place, and life is lived solely for pictures."

Rather than Valhalla, this sounded like the drudgery of King Solomon's Mines with royalty digging as well as wearing their diamonds.

"I work such long hours," wrote Lillian Gish, hailed as "the World's Darling" and "the Duse and Bernhardt of the Screen"

LIVING FOR OTHERS

*At home with the Gishes —
Mother, daughters
and Mary Pickford*

Lillian in BROKEN BLOSSOMS

JESSE L. LASKY
Feature Play Co
·HOLLYWOOD·

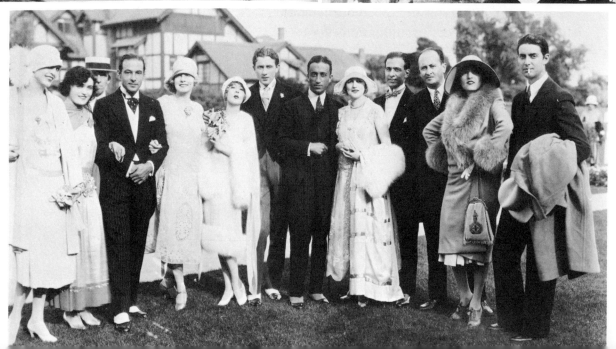

for her portrayal of the pitiful Limehouse waif in *Broken Blossoms.* "Sometimes I don't even see Mother for days. Can you imagine us living in the same house and hardly seeing one another? . . . I certainly was not made to be famous, it is beginning to get on my nerves."

Cecil B. De Mille and friends

Greta Garbo, whose arrival on the Hollywood scene signaled the beginning of Miss Gish's eclipse, said flatly, "No one making films can be happy."

In Paris it was live and let live. In Hollywood the adoring multitudes who stripped every rosebush in greater Los Angeles and strewed the petals in the path of their current favorite were the same who scattered carpet tacks and broken glass in the way of cherubic Mary Miles Minter and cuddly Mabel Normand when the living got too easy, who dropped the guillotine on the neck of Fatty Arbuckle's career when his penchant for wild parties ended in a manslaughter charge for the gruesome death of actress Virginia Rappe.

The money was good, but the pressure was awful. The combination of the two did in Wally Reid, Olive Thomas, Alma Rubens, Jeanne Eagels, Barbara LaMarr, Valentino himself, whose gleaming, smoothly muscled exterior hid a fatal lesion within.

Their tragedies had no resonance. However abjectly adored the stars had been, there were always others to take their place. They made the supreme sacrifice for masterpieces more ephemeral than the Mazda bulbs that heralded their arrival on Main Street: *Restless Souls, What's Your Hurry, The Dancin' Fool, Madame Sphinx, The Flapper, Man, Woman and Sin, Souls for Sale, Heart of a Siren, The Sheik, The Eagle, The Son of the Sheik.*

Mae Murray's wedding day

"*Be proud of corn,*" said Cecil B. De Mille — "the acknowledged messiah of sunken bathtubs, ermine-tailed boudoir gowns, plush footmen, and tigerskin rugs," according to a contemporary detractor, as well as one of the half-dozen men behind the cameras who told the gods and goddesses of Hollywood what they could and could not do. "*Corn is soul, corn is that which makes you cry and laugh. Corn is all humanity. Yes, my pictures have corn and I am proud of it.*"

De Mille's proud corn included *Male and Female, Forbidden Fruit, The Golden Bed, The Volga Boatmen, The Ten Commandments,* and *The King of Kings* — during the filming of which his entrance on the set, resplendent with megaphone, riding crop and puttees, was greeted by a ten-stop organ playing "Onward Christian Soldiers."

It wasn't quite all work and no play in the diamond mines and cornfields of Hollywood. There were occasional good times — opportunities to display the good things that five thousand, ten thousand, twenty thousand a week could buy. And there were mistresses of ceremonies here as well.

As everyone in Paris sensed that the Left Bank belonged to Gertrude and the Right to Elsa, in Hollywood the hills were Mary's, the beach Marion's. Mary Pickford and Marion Davies — America's and Mr. William Randolph Hearst's Sweethearts.

At Pickfair, the large nondescript house with its wide lawns and unscalable walls, Miss Pickford played hostess to anyone of consequence from the outside world. "This was Hollywood's most august social tribunal," wrote Lloyd Morris, "and its atmosphere suggested the remoteness and exclusiveness traditionally associated with royalty. An invitation to dine at Pickfair was an accolade, the local equivalent of a command to Buckingham Palace."

Scott and Zelda came to dine and "marvel at Mary Pickford's dynamic subjugation of life." So did Mr. and Mrs. Henry Ford, Bernard Shaw and Queen Marie of Romania.

In the ninety-room beach cottage of Marion Davies at Santa Monica — with its two swimming pools, three dining rooms, gold-ceilinged drawing room and private theater — things tended to be less formal. But the caliber of the guests was just as impressive: Winston Churchill, Somerset Maugham, Scott and Zelda, Bernard Shaw, Queen Marie. As alternatives to seaside infor-

PICKFAIR: *A pool for two with canoe*

mality Miss Davies had her fourteen-room dressing room at the MGM lot, which, according to Lady Diana Cooper, who was raised in a genuine English castle, was "as big as a church"; or she could call on the formidable facilities of "The Enchanted Hill," San Simeon, the castle ranch of her friend and protector William Randolph Hearst, with a 240,000-acre front yard for privacy.

Against these impressive attractions Mary weighed her fame, her fortune, and her husband Douglas Fairbanks, a twenty-four-carat full-time movie star in his own right.

There were other distractions besides those afforded by Hollywood's grandest dames. On "collegiate" Friday nights at the Cocoanut Grove, Joan Crawford (Mary Pickford's step-daughter-in-law to be) won cup after loving cup for her incomparable Charleston, until genuine collegians finally objected that she wasn't one of them.

There were excursions to Laguna Beach, whose rocky coves and turquoise waters rivaled the Mediterranean's, or to Coronado where, on the veranda of the largest wooden structure in the world, Boston Brahmins rocked, and in the surf Mack Sennett girls stepped daintily on stingrays and dodged an occasional shark. Across the border in Mexico was Agua Caliente, famous for its mineral waters, its gambling and "the longest bar in the world." Across the desert was Palm Springs, even sunnier than sunny Hollywood; and down Sunset Boulevard and up the coast was Malibu, a colony of shacks reached by a narrow dirt road, but of a Sunday, according to *Vanity Fair*, glittering to the heavens with the Rolls-Royces, Minervas, and Hispano-Suizas of the resident stars and their guests.

But early Monday morning each Rolls, Minerva and Hispano-Suiza purred back through its particular "abandon hope" studio gate for another concentrated six-day stretch of work.

Marion Davies (seated): A 240,000-acre front yard

The talkies and the Crash descended upon primitive and feudal Hollywood in rapid succession. But fragile and phantasmagoric as the town may have seemed, it sustained the double blow. In fact, a renaissance of sorts followed.

The hegemony of Miss Pickford and Miss Davies was somewhat weakened; a great many of their dearest friends were swept to oblivion by the necessity of talking. They were easily replaced.

If the Crash stripped Paris of many of its most glittering ornaments, Hollywood was the richer for it. The refugees from the City of Light arrived in hordes upon the Pacific Coast.

Elsa came — by special invitation of David Selznick — and cocked a critical eye at Hollywood's social life:

"I had gone there expecting to see parties that reflected the stock-in-trade of the movies — glamour. Instead, I found the same attitude toward parties that European peasants had for baths. It was something to be done methodically every Saturday night . . . there was only one place to go on any given Saturday night and everyone went there like so many prisoners released on a twenty-four-hour parole."

As if by magic her old playmates appeared, to help her liven things up. Noel Coward and George Gershwin, Cole Porter, Stravinsky, Rubinstein and Heifetz . . . Curiosity, climate and cash exercised their fatal attraction.

Gertrude Stein showed up as well, delivered a lecture and had dinner in Beverly Hills with Charlie Chaplin, Anita Loos, and Dashiell Hammett: . . . "they wanted to know how I had succeeded in getting so much publicity, I said by having a small audience, I said if you have a big audience you have no publicity, this did seem to worry them and naturally it would worry them they wanted the publicity and the big audience. . . ."

George Antheil, out to do movie music for Cecil B. De Mille, took up residence at the Hollywood-Franklin Hotel and rediscovered the Left Bank. "Jammed with genial movie bit players, too-bright-eyed young actresses waiting for a break, movie mothers with ridiculously frumped children, writers, radio announcers, and such-like, the place had an atmosphere of the old Latin Quarter of Paris . . . I felt at home from the very beginning."

Refugee Coward

Even native-born Parisians came, notably Maurice Chevalier in his bat-wing bow tie, straw hat, and watermelon grin.

The idle rich drifted west. Vincent Astor's yacht *Nourmahal* tied up at San Pedro while he investigated quaint native customs. Prince Serge Obolensky, Raymond Guest, Jock Whitney shared the steam baths of Chaplin, Fairbanks and Selznick. Alfred Vanderbilt and Ginger Rogers gave a roller skating party together.

The Gish and Talmadge sisters gave way to the Youngs, the Bennetts and the Lanes. Blondes in white satin replaced brunettes in ermine-tailed boudoir gowns and frizzy redheads in fringe. Skirts dropped, bobs lengthened, bosoms, waists, and hips reappeared. Now it was Jean Harlow in *Hell's Angels*, Irene Dunne in *Cimarron*, Mae West in *She Done Him Wrong*, Rogers and Astaire in *Top Hat*, Colbert and Gable in *It Happened One Night*, Gable and Laughton in *Mutiny on the Bounty* and Gable and Leigh in *Gone With the Wind*. The names had changed, but Hollywood was more than ever the capital of the world.

As he had Paris, Scott Fitzgerald hit Hollywood at its peak, and after. He found the shiny apple, and the worm. "A mining town in Lotus land," he observed. "Under the moon the back lot was thirty acres of fairyland — not because the locations really looked like African jungles and French châteaux and schooners at anchor and Broadway by night, but because they looked like the torn picture-books of childhood, like fragments of stories dancing in an open fire. I never lived in a house with an attic, but a back lot must be something like that, and at night of course in an enchanted, distorted way, it all comes true."

He also found alcohol. At a party of the reigning hostess of the moment and his boss, Norma Shearer and Irving Thalberg, he insulted the guests, sang a sophomoric comic song and was fired within the week. Desperate, he tried again and again. *Three Comrades, Winter Carnival, Gone With the Wind* — the Fitzgerald versions wouldn't do. Others were called in to take over. A year after *Gone With the Wind* opened and proved itself the cinema event of the double decade, fifteen months after Hitler marched into Poland, the body of Francis Scott Key Fitzgerald was exposed in a Hollywood mortuary.

"He was laid out to look like a cross between a floor-walker and a wax dummy in the window of a two-pants tailor," wrote Frank Scully, one of the few old friends who bothered to pay his respects. "But in Technicolor. Not a line showed on his face. His hair was parted slightly to one side. None of it was gray.

"Until you reached his hands, this looked strictly like an A-production in peace and security. Realism began at his extremities. His hands were horribly wrinkled and thin, the only proof left after death that for all the props of youth, he actually had suffered and died an old man."

Of all the people who knew both Paris and Hollywood in the Years Between, none bridged the gap between the two cities so significantly as Fitzgerald, seeing the beauties of one, the fascination of the other, seeking out their weaknesses, recording them, taking advantage of them, underlining them with his own.

Listening to Fitzgerald one suddenly realized how little grownups had counted in the capitals of the Years Between. Paris had been the Mecca of the immature — of the young artist establishing his talent, of the lost generation finding itself, of Peter Pans needing the shock of Radio dropping from 505 to 36 to bring them back from Never Land. Hollywood had been the Medina of the infantile. "Probably never in history has so immature a group been accorded such luster, such sanctions, and such incomes," said Leo Rosten, come to observe scientifically the film capital's manners and mores as the Years Between drew to a close.

With Fitzgerald old in his coffin and the world going up in flames all around, Hollywood would never be the same — although its favored citizens would continue for a while to behave as though it were. Paris, always the same, would never give itself quite so easily or cheaply to youth again.

It was time for everyone to grow up — quick . . . or perish.

IL DUCE AND BAPU

THE LEADER AND FATHER—Mussolini and Gandhi.

The men and their careers manifested both the political and the human extremes of the Years Between. Gandhi, the little fellow in the sheet, as wizened as a monkey, frail, self-effacing, soft-spoken, unabashedly spiritual and infinitely durable; and Mussolini, the gorilla in uniform, all muscle and ego, chin and barrel chest, arrogantly carnal, foul-mouthed, expedient, and, in the end, pathetically vulnerable.

They met once, in 1931, when Gandhi spent forty-eight hours traversing Italy en route from London to India. The Hindu, sipping goat's milk, spinning and praying as he went, had wished to meet the head of the Catholic Church, but according to a *New York Times* headline, GANDHI'S SCANT GARB BARS AUDIENCE WITH POPE. He was allotted ten minutes with Il Duce.

"I noticed that he had so arranged things about him that a visitor would easily get stricken with terror," Gandhi reported later. "The walls of the passage, through which one has to pass to reach him are all over studded with various types of swords and other weapons. In his own room, too, there is not a single picture or anything of that kind on the walls, but they are covered with weapons.

"He has the eyes of a cat. . . . They moved about in every direction as if in constant rotation. The visitor would totally succumb before the awe of his gaze like a rat running directly into the mouth of a cat out of mere fright. I was not to be dazed like that."

There is no record of Mussolini's reaction to the spidery little man except that he escorted him to the door, an unwonted courtesy to guests, and arranged that the great pacifist review the Balilla Musketeers, a corps of Italian youngsters trained in the arts of war. The eight- and nine-year-olds in panoply complimented Gandhi with a cannonade.

"A house of cards," Gandhi labeled Italian Fascism; and four years later he commented on the single most conspicuous act of Mussolini's career, his invasion of Abyssinia: "If the Abyssinians

had adopted the attitude of nonviolence of the strong, that is, the nonviolence which breaks to pieces but never bends, Mussolini would have had no interest in Abyssinia. Thus if they had simply said: 'You are welcome to reduce us to dust and ashes, but you will not find one Abyssinian ready to co-operate with you,' what could Mussolini have done?"

Had Mussolini heard those words, he, no doubt, would have considered their speaker insane. There was little doubt as to Gandhi's opinion of Il Duce's mental health.

They were both bald; they were both sometime journalists; and the accidents of history molded them both into aggressive nationalists.

All men have something in common.

In 1919, Benito Mussolini was thirty-six, a socialist revolutionary schoolteacher and agitator, a former pacifist, anarchist, vagrant, with a reputation for troublemaking and turning his coat. On the twenty-third of March, following the armistice, he addressed the first meeting of *Fasci* in Milan — a few dozen thugs and malcontents with revolutionary leanings.

"I said," said Mussolini, " 'The proletariat needs a bath of blood' — it has had a bath of blood — one that has lasted three years. 'The proletariat needs a day of glory, a day to be remembered,' I said also. It has had a thousand such days."

Behind him were the writings of Hegel, Nietzsche, Sorel, and D'Annunzio, the example of Lenin. Blending them all together, he fashioned his own personal version of the Superman: "I am a leader who leads, not a leader who follows. I go — now and above all — against the current and never abandon myself to it, and I watch always, above all, for the changing winds to swell the sails of my destiny."

The winds that blew him onward, as they were to blow his

Mussolini: A day of glory

counterparts in other lands, were the discontent of an abandoned soldiery, a hard-pressed middle class, and aristocrats and industrialists who, fearful of a loss of wealth and privilege should Bolshevism prevail, backed anyone who promised to protect them against it.

Contempt for Wilson and his Fourteen Points went without saying: "The man from across the Atlantic, with his hard jaw, rosy coloring . . . and flat feet," with his mouth "full of false words and false teeth." Mussolini borrowed the sentiments and phrasing from his idol D'Annunzio, who had just "pulled the beards of the three old idiots" of Versailles by setting up a poetic dictatorship in the Adriatic port of Fiume. D'Annunzio's style in action as well as diction helped set Mussolini's own.

"Liberty today is no longer the chaste and severe virgin for whom fought and died the generations of the first half of the past century," said Mussolini, who as late as 1915 had still been a pacifist, and whose war record was of questionable distinction. "For the youths of today, intrepid, eager, stern, who envisage the dawn of the new era, there are other words which exercise a more potent fascination, and these words are: Order, Hierarchy, Discipline. . . ."

Order, Hierarchy, and Discipline included truncheons, castor oil, hand grenades and flaming torches with which the Fascist youth intimidated and purged the opposition. In a few months the fifty-odd who had made up the original Fascist "bundle" in Milan multiplied to 300,000 in 2000 bundles across the land. Fascist raids and riots resulted in thousands killed and injured.

"Either the government of the country is handed over to us peaceably, or we shall take it by force, marching on Rome, and engaging in a struggle to the death with the politicians now in power." At the end of October, 1922, Mussolini's minions set out for the Eternal City. And on the thirtieth of the month, Mussolini, who had loitered behind awaiting the outcome, followed by train, self-consciously crossing the Rubicon, to accept from the King the portfolio of prime minister.

Dictatorial powers, his private militia and secret police, soon followed; and in 1924 the last legal and articulate opposition dis-

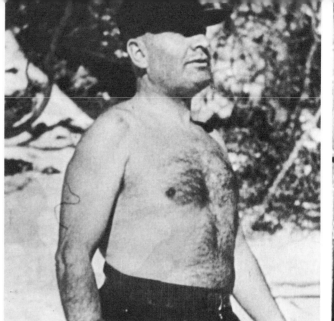
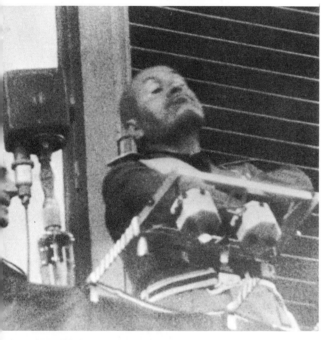

appeared when the Socialist Senator Giacomo Matteotti was murdered by Fascist assassins.

"Yes, I am obsessed by this wild desire," Mussolini confessed to a lady friend. "It consumes my whole being. I want to make a mark on my era with my will, like a lion with its claw! A mark like *this!*"

"And, as with a claw," she related ecstatically, "he scratched the covering of a chair-back from end to end!"

Fingernails across velour . . . To the hypnotized female it seemed a grand, symbolic gesture. And yet the back of a firm hand could erase it in an instant.

FOR MY PART, I PREFER 50,000 RIFLES TO FIVE MILLION VOTES.

HE WHO HAS STEEL HAS BREAD.

NOTHING AGAINST THE STATE, NOTHING OUTSIDE THE STATE.

BETTER TO LIVE ONE DAY AS A LION THAN A HUNDRED YEARS A SHEEP.

NOTHING IS EVER WON IN HISTORY WITHOUT BLOODSHED.

BELIEVE, OBEY, FIGHT.

MUSSOLINI IS ALWAYS RIGHT.

From the Valle d'Aosta to the beaches of Gela, the slogans appeared stenciled on walls by the faithful and the opportunistic.

Playwright Luigi Pirandello gave his blessing. Composer Giacomo Puccini was made a Senator. Arturo Toscanini was a party member until he was told he must play the Fascist anthem "Giovanezza" at all concerts. Marconi became a Marquis, and D'Annunzio was dubbed the "Prince of Monte Nevoso" with his own castle prison jutting into beautiful Lake Garda. Mascagni was converted.

The new Academy of sixty chosen by Mussolini had members who got a salary, were called "Your Excellency," and were permitted free first-class travel by rail. They were tricked out in mock-antique uniforms complete with plumed hats and gilt swords; the hat of the president of the Academy was ornamented with ostrich feathers.

It was "the time of the carrot and the stick," said Mussolini; and very few could resist. The trains ran on time. The Pontine Marshes were drained. But the price of bread rose and wages dropped. "Fortunately," Mussolini remarked, "the Italian people were not accustomed to eat much and therefore feel the privation less acutely than others."

Liberty, labeled strumpet, expired.

"Today people have not so much time to think as they used to have," Mussolini told biographer historian Emil Ludwig, who paid him a visit shortly after Gandhi's and was given somewhat more time. "The capacity of the modern man for faith is illimitable. When the masses are like wax in my hands, when I stir their faith, or when I mingle with them and am almost crushed by them, I feel myself part of them. All the same there persists in me a certain feeling of aversion, like that which the modeler feels for the clay he is molding. Does not the sculptor sometimes smash the block of marble into fragments because he cannot shape it to represent the vision he has conceived? Now and then, this crude matter rebels against the creator."

In answer to the query, Can a dictator be loved?, he answered, "Yes, provided that the masses fear him at the time time. The crowd loves strong men. The crowd is like a woman."

Playtime with the Dolfusses

Claretta Petacci at home

Mussolini was rumored to have a desperate effect on women. Lady Oxford found his voice thrilling. His cat's eyes were supposed to have an impact simultaneously paralyzing and aphrodisiac that facilitated his conquests. The Italians, would-be wolves from the days of Romulus and Remus, clucked and leered and reveled in the tales of Il Duce's prowess and the resulting kindergarten full of illegitimate offspring. It spoke well for all Italian males that their leader was so potent.

Nor were children exempt from the legend of his magnetism. In their schoolbooks they read:

> The eyes of the Duce are on every one of you, no one can say what is the meaning of that look on his face. It is an eagle opening its wings and rising into space. It is a flame that searches out your heart to light there a vermilion fire. Who can resist that burning eye, darting out its arrows? But do not be afraid; for you those arrows will change into rays of joy.

He had admirers who did not have the motive of patriotism, sex, or childishness to prompt their approval. Winston Churchill, who deplored Gandhi and was revolted by "the nauseating and humiliating spectacle of this one-time Inner Temple lawyer, now

Total mobilization

The first meeting

seditious fakir, striding half naked up the steps of the Viceroy's palace, there to negotiate and to parley on equal terms with the representative of the King-Emperor," found Mussolini all charm and gentleness.

Churchill's affection for Mussolini soon dwindled. In 1935 the Italians invaded Ethiopia and aggravated the statesman's concern for the same Empire which Gandhi had so sorely offended.

The Ethiopian War gained nothing for Il Duce except perhaps a momentary heightening of national pride, and the illusion of a new Empire for Italy under his leadership.

But this cheap success — only 1537 Italians had lost their lives in conquering a land four times as big as their own — was actually a step in Mussolini's hitherto imperceptible decline.

Already Adolf Hitler, Il Duce's nemesis-to-be and one-time sincere admirer and slavish imitator, had defied his teacher by arranging the murder of Mussolini's *protégé*, Austrian Chancellor Dollfuss. "The Wilhelmstrasse is delighted," William Shirer noted in his *Berlin Diary*, the day after the Ethiopian war was declared. "Either Mussolini will stumble and get himself so heavily involved in Africa that he will be greatly weakened in Europe, whereupon Hitler can seize Austria, hitherto protected by the Duce; or he will win, defying France and Britain, and

*Ethiopian Emperor
Haile Selassie*

. . . and his troops

thereupon be ripe for a tie-up with Hitler against the Western democracies. Either way, Hitler wins."

Either way, Mussolini lost. Eventually, Hitler won *both* ways.

"It means inevitable ruin," D'Annunzio commented on the increasing bond between Mussolini and Hitler. Mussolini ignored the warning, and for each meeting had new and fancier uniforms designed so that he might strut and fret more magnificently beside the monster he had helped create and who at the moment possessed the blue-print for his precursor's destruction.

At each juncture Mussolini was outclassed. The Italian participation in the Spanish Civil War was a joyless drain, from which Il Duce managed to draw not even the questionable benefit of training his troops and strategists in modern warfare. Hitler, who invested fewer men, less time and less money, made capital of his involvement. The Austrian upstart, who had, according to legend, been refused a coveted autographed photograph of Il Duce when he was still an unknown political crackpot in Munich, now set the pace for his one-time idol.

Il Duce permitted Hitler his Austrian *Anschluss* in 1938. That same year, he agreed to adopt Hitler's policy of anti-Semitism. The next year a formal military alliance was consummated — and Mussolini's doom was sealed.

Franco reviews Italian troops in Spain

Hitler plays host

By the time Hitler invaded Poland, Mussolini was complaining that his partner was sending him only perfunctory notes telling him whenever Germany had taken over another country. It was the whine of a prematurely old man, bewildered by the decay of his own legend. The ulcer and the syphilis that could not be admitted . . . The fall from horseback that no newspaper could report . . . The burning light in his study to give Rome the impression that he was ceaselessly at work, when he was actually asleep or lying beside his mistress, Clara Petacci . . . Self-indulgence, self-delusion, had made him old, lonely, ailing, complaining of the lack of respect of his fantastically successful pupil and labeling himself "The most disobeyed man in history."

The war that Hitler made should have been Mussolini's, the vindication of all that he had claimed for himself, the demonstration of his tenet that war alone brings all human energies to their highest state of tension, and stamps with the seal of nobility the nations which dare to face it. Instead it found him and his country unprepared, unenthusiastic, unheroic. He waited before joining in the conflict, his cat's eyes shifting from one side to the other, trying to make out the winner. Finally he chose the wrong man.

Three years of multiplying miseries, of public humiliation and disgrace, separated Mussolini from his death, the desecration of his corpse, and his burial in unknown, unconsecrated ground. The adumbrator of most of the twentieth century's dictators left scarcely more trace behind him than his nails on the velvet chairback he had clawed twenty years before.

Claretta and Benito, 1945

"The children of violence will commit suicide and perish, unless they turn away from violence," was Gandhi's judgment on mankind's favorite pastime.

In 1919, when Mussolini was advocating blood-baths and the manifold glories of war as specifics for what ailed his fellow countrymen, Gandhi, a British-trained Hindu lawyer in his fiftieth year who had spent his young manhood fighting for racial equality in South Africa, was urging nonviolence on his fellow

Indians as a way to attain their nationalist goals. The writings of Tolstoi, Thoreau, Ruskin, Emerson, the Sermon on the Mount and the Bhagavad-Gita had nurtured him. The examples of Krishna, the Buddha, Christ had given him strength. The technique with which he hoped to replace bloodshed he called *Satyagraha*, "the force that is born of Truth and Love, or nonviolence."

In 1919, almost to the day that Mussolini addressed the first small Fascist meeting in Milan, Gandhi took his first overt action against the British Crown in India by urging his compatriots to participate in a voluntary work stoppage protesting the Indians' lack of liberty.

It turned out to be the beginning of a struggle which has yet to end.

"We hope to reverse the process, and by our action show that physical force is nothing compared to moral force, and that moral force never fails," he told the puzzled British Viceroy.

Elsewhere he affirmed his belief in "the law of the final supremacy of spirit over matter, of liberty and love over brute force."

One result of the work stoppages, which at his prompting swept the subcontinent, was the Amritsar massacre in 1919, in which over ten thousand unarmed Indians trapped in a littered clearing walled-in by buildings were shot down by British troops. Sixteen thousand, six hundred and fifty rounds were fired. Three hundred and seventy-nine people were killed; one thousand, one hundred and thirty-seven wounded. The massacre decided Gandhi, heretofore reluctant, to enter politics. He became president of the All-India Home Rule League. His recommendations for retaliation were to nonco-operate, to passively resist, refuse to pay taxes, to burn all European clothes and spin and weave the rough cloth to replace them — *not* to fight.

While Mussolini and his followers were putting on their fancy

Gandhi and his troops . . .

NEXT PAGE: *India, home of nonviolence —
from the salt march to Independence*

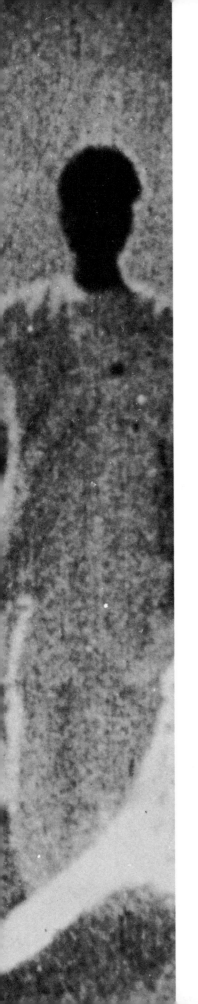

dress and ornamenting themselves with feathers, Gandhi resolved henceforth to wear nothing but a loincloth of homespun.

FORGIVENESS IS MORE MANLY THAN PUNISHMENTS.

NONVIOLENCE IS THE LAW OF OUR SPECIES AS VIOLENCE IS THE LAW OF THE BRUTE.

IF INDIA TAKES UP THE DOCTRINE OF THE SWORD SHE MAY GAIN MOMENTARY VICTORY, BUT THEN INDIA WILL CEASE TO BE THE PRIDE OF MY HEART.

To graduates of the playing fields of Eton and Sandhurst, these sentiments seemed sheerest poppycock. "I thought I would be doing a jolly lot of good," said Brigadier General Dyer, the man who gave the order to fire at Amritsar.

Against Mussolini's doctrine of *Believe, obey, fight,* or its Empire equivalent *Theirs not to reason why, Theirs but to do and die,* Gandhi put *Peace, nonviolence, suffering.* In 1922 Italy's government had been handed over to Mussolini lock, stock and barrel, to do with what he willed — the same year, Gandhi was sentenced to six years in prison for attempting to overthrow His Majesty's government.

While Mussolini brandished his fist from balconies and bellowed words to amaze and confound his credulous listeners, Gandhi fasted and wept in his efforts to unify Moslem and Hindu India and set it free.

Farmer and city dweller

"The way of truth is also always the way of peace," persisted Gandhi. "Untruthfulness, on the other hand, is the mother of violence. A man who strives after verity can never remain violent for any length of time. He will soon realize that he needs not violence, and he will discover that the slightest traces of violence bar him from reaching his goal, which is truth. The truth of a few will prove more important than the untruth of millions."

Upon his release from jail in 1924 he abandoned political office to help "purify" India and prepare it for its future trials and responsibilities. He had faith in the reconciliation of India's irreconcilables, "because I believe in human nature."

On March 2, 1930 Gandhi sent a letter to the Viceroy of India. It said in part:

Dear Friend,

Before embarking on Civil Disobedience and taking the risk I have dreaded to take all these years, I would fain approach you and find a way out.

My personal faith is absolutely clear. I cannot intentionally hurt anything that lives, much less human beings, even though they may do the greatest wrong to me and mine. Whilst, therefore, I hold the British rule to be a curse, I do not intend harm to a single Englishman or to any legitimate interest he may have in India. . . .

The poor and the rich

And why do I regard the British rule as a curse?

It has impoverished the dumb millions by a system of progressive exploitation and by a ruinous expensive military and civil administration which the country can never afford.

It has reduced us politically to serfdom . . . it has degraded us spiritually. . . .

Nothing but organized nonviolence can check the organized violence of the British government. . . .

If you cannot see your way to deal with these evils and if my letter makes no appeal to your heart, on the eleventh day of this month I shall proceed . . . to disregard the provisions of the Salt Laws. . . .

The Viceroy sent a perfunctory reply; and on the twelfth day of the month Gandhi and seventy-eight of his followers started to walk toward the sea. In twenty-four days they walked two hundred miles, and by the time they reached the coast their numbers had grown to thousands. Gandhi walked to the water and returned with a lump of salt left on the sand by the waves. The gesture was the crest of the tide of defiance started at Amritsar.

Soon up and down the seacoast every peasant was wading out to sea to make salt. Sixty thousand were arrested, including Gandhi.

They got Gandhi in jail in India [wrote Will Rogers back in the U.S.A.]. He preached "Liberty without violence." He swore all his followers "to truth and constant poverty." He wanted nothing for himself, not even the ordinary comforts. He believed in "prayer and renunciation." Well, naturally a man that bold couldn't run at large these days. They figured that a crazy man like that was liable to get other people to wanting those fanatical things. The whole thing just gives you a pretty fair idea of what would happen to our Saviour if he would come on earth today. Why, say, he wouldn't last near as long as he did then. Civilization has got past "truth and poverty and renunciation" and all that old junk. Throw those nuts in jail.

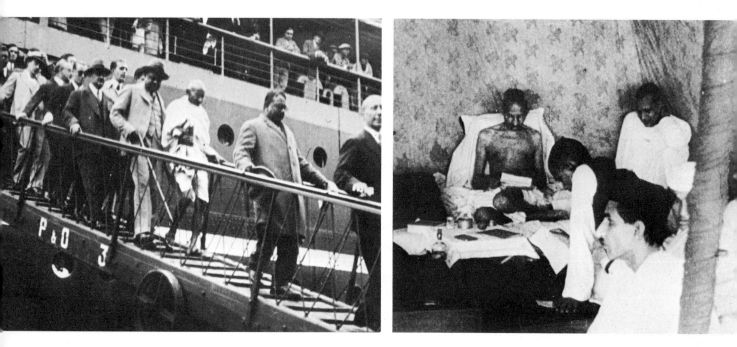

Gandhi was released from jail at the beginning of 1931 and met with the Viceroy on equal terms. In August he set out for London for further conferences. In the slums, where he insisted upon living, the Cockneys called him Uncle Gandhi. The press made flip remarks about his dress and physique and compared him to Mickey Mouse. He had offers to appear in vaudeville and the circus. Charlie Chaplin asked to meet him, and, although Gandhi didn't think much of actors, he consented when he heard the great comedian had started life as an East End waif. George Bernard Shaw paid his respects; David Lloyd George had him down to his country place; and he went for tea at Buckingham Palace wearing the same outfit that would later keep him from seeing the Pope. Churchill snubbed him.

Despite his universal popularity, the talks were inconclusive. Within a week of his return to India he was back in jail.

Gandhi spent a total of 2338 days behind bars during his lifetime. But his power in jail became as formidable as his traveling, preaching, teaching. In jail he began his Epic Fast, his fast to the death to better the condition of India's millions of untouch-

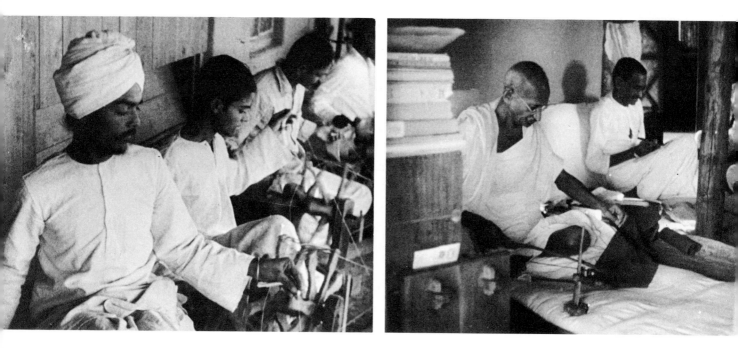

ables. On the sixth day, when he was so weak he could not speak, his program was adopted by his fellow Indians, and by the British. The Epic Fast was one of sixteen that Gandhi undertook in his lifetime. For many, his followers had special names: the Great Fast, the Self-purification Fast, the Historic Fast. In many, he announced his intention to fast to the death rather than to give up his purpose. "So long as we let ourselves be influenced by the fear of death, we can never attain to freedom." Gandhi thus explained his willingness to risk the extinction of his fragile body.

Although his countrymen early granted him the title of Mahatma — "Great Soul" — and Bapu — "Father" — and looked on him with that combination of awe and affectionate familiarity that only a saint and holy man commands, their adulation embarrassed him. "I make no claim to superhuman powers. I am as subject to error as the weakest among us. My services have many limitations. It is a million times better that I should be the laughing-stock of the world than that I should act insincerely toward myself. The country will have gained by my humiliation and confession of error."

In the Thirties, when Mussolini was planning his future forays into Ethiopia and Spain, Gandhi devoted himself to improving the lot of his fellow Hindus and increasing their understanding and love for those of disparate religion and race that surrounded them. His interest in India's independence came second to his concern for the welfare of the untouchables, the relationship of Hindu to Moslem, the conditions in rural villages. He walked barefoot from community to community, teaching and preaching, helping the poor, and the ignorant. "When I succeed in ridding the villages of their poverty, I have won Swaraj [home rule]."

In 1939, India's independence once more became paramount. Gandhi began his Historic Fast to hasten it:

"Even if it means the loss of my life, which, after all, at the age of seventy has no insurance value, I should be most willing to give it in order to secure the due performance of a sacred promise."

"My faith is brightest in the midst of impenetrable darkness," Gandhi said as he saw the European war coming nearer. "Neither God nor nonviolence is impotent. Impotence is in men. I must try on, without losing faith."

The sacred promise for which Gandhi had fasted was not fulfilled for eight more years, two of which Gandhi spent in jail at the instigation of his old antagonist, Churchill. When independence came it was under circumstances that caused Gandhi to mourn rather than rejoice. There was violence — violence this time not between British and Indian but between Moslem and Hindu; violence, misery, displacement, death. He was given two more years to do his best to heal the wounds that Indian inflicted

Gandhi on the march

upon Indian; then he himself, on his way to afternoon prayers, was murdered — a victim of the fanaticism that corrupted both sides.

Twenty million mourners watched the train depart from Delhi carrying Gandhi's ashes to the Ganges. Thousands threw themselves bodily in the Sacred River when the remains were scattered upon its waters.

"Bapu has gone out of our lives," said his political heir, Nehru. "The light has gone out and there is darkness everywhere."

It was not quite true. Along the tracks to Allahabad, where crowds collected to watch the funeral train pass by, the cry went up *"Mahatma Gandhi ki-jai!"* ("Victory to Mahatma Gandhi!") and *"Mahatma Gandhi ancar hai!"* ("Mahatma Gandhi will never die!")

Meanwhile in Italy, weather and the hand of man had almost obliterated the bold capitals that had blazoned forth the power of Il Duce on farm walls, *cantoneria*, warehouses and sidings. However, here and there could still be made out the inscriptions: *Better to live one day as a lion than a hundred years a sheep. . . . He who has steel has bread. . . . Mussolini is always right.*

A VIOLENT FLOWERING

THE BIG EVENT of the Berlin theatrical season of 1927 was a play with the effervescent title *Hoppla, Wir Leben (Whoopee! Such Is Life!)*. Written by Ernst Toller, one of Germany's leading dramatists; staged by the brilliant theatrical innovator Erwin Piscator, it was played in a towering jungle gym of iron tubing. The lighting was bizarre; the sound effects startling and weird. And there was a motion picture screen at stage rear which flashed on at strategic moments to make the total effect even more overwhelming. "An elegant bejeweled public paid up to twenty-five dollars for a seat to mingle with students and workers," reported an eyewitness. "One segment of the audience began to sing the 'Internationale' after the final curtain had come down, while the other half called for their chauffeurs to be taken to the Adlon Hotel for supper or to one of the many cabarets."

The Adlon and the cabarets were equally renowned; the Adlon for its luxury, and the ostentation of its guests; the cabarets for the ruthless sarcasm of their *conférenciers*. These men, half entertainers, half anthropologists, stopped at nothing to shock, inform and amuse. Existing in a limbo between the bejeweled patrons who could afford to join their audiences and the masses who couldn't, but with whom they had common cause, they were the intellectual gadflies of contemporary Berlin. And Berlin was the Athens of the Weimar Republic and of what one German critic called "the Periclean Age of German arts and letters."

German music and drama, German architecture, German fiction for the moment seemed to pace the world. In Berlin three major opera houses worked full time (in a single year Germany staged world premieres of sixty new operas). There were dozens of theaters purveying wildly experimental fare. Artists, composers, writers all flourished, patronized and praised, criticized and derided by rich and poor, privileged and underprivileged alike.

And here in Erwin Piscator's theater the rich and the radical, the student and the industrialist, sat side by side. It could have been an indication of health, resilience, of recovery from the horrid aftermath of World War I, of a remarkable tolerance and adaptability to a new era.

It was, alas, anything but.

Karl Thomas, the hero of *Whoopee! Such Is Life!* was no Jazz Age man-about-town enjoying his newfound freedom. He was a humorless veteran of the German revolutions of 1918–1919, released after eight years in an insane asylum to face the Germany of 1927 with the stunned objectivity of Rip Van Winkle wakened after his long sleep. He saw around him not gaiety, vitality and hope, but despair and doom: the hollow, haunted look of the jaded idealist; the skeleton beneath the skin of the profiteer and his painted, jewel-bedizened consort. "The faces in the street, in the Underground. . . . dreadful! I've never noticed before how few people have faces. Lumps of flesh, most of them, blown up with worry and conceit."

A Periclean Age . . . illusion and reality

"What are we today in comparison with the mob?" complained a corrupt aristocrat in the play. "Nobodies. And in society, umpteen miles behind the *nouveau riche*."

"You have only to snuff the atmosphere of the industrial world!" said a *nouveau riche*. "I'd advise you to put your money on a national dictator."

A faceless loudspeaker barked the play's sinister message at the audience with heavy irony:

> Unrest in India . . . Unrest in China . . . Unrest in Africa. . . . Paris! Paris! Houbigant the fashionable perfume. Bucharest! Bucharest! Famine in Romania. Berlin! Berlin! Elegant ladies delight in green wigs. New York! New York! The largest bombing plane in the world invented — capable of destroying European capitals in a second. . . . Wireless Stations of the World — the latest slogan — "Whoopee! Such Is Life!"

In such an environment, "There are only two chances left," the hero concluded; "to hang oneself, or to change the world." Before the curtain fell and the audience dispersed to their fashionable cabarets and revolutionary cabals, their hall bedrooms and their country houses, the hero made his choice. He hung himself.

His action in a way epitomized the sad history of Germany's first experiment in democracy, the Weimar Republic, which was then enjoying its greatest prosperity — and foreshadowed its unhappy end.

Born of despair and expediency, the Weimar Republic was declared by an uneasy alliance of moderates and militarists in November 1918, principally to prevent the setting up of a German Union of Soviets in the ruins of the defeated Reich. Once it was in existence, it was mercilessly harassed by extremists from both Right and Left, who observed its attempts at moderation and compromise with hostile contempt. Continually reminded of a guilt that it was incapable of acknowledging, hampered by an endemic lack of humor, the German nation undertook its experiment in democracy awkwardly and resentfully. For thirteen years this sickly government pursued its listless course with little encouragement within or without its borders. Finally, thanks to the connivance of its two supposedly irreconcilable antagonists, and to the exhaustion of its meager political energies, it collapsed, in a hysterical fit of tribal defiance and egotism. Its ruins furnished the kindling for the greatest conflagration the world has yet known.

Germany came out of World War I with 1,600,000 killed, 203,000 missing, 4,054,000 wounded and disabled. 705,000 civilians were dead of malnutrition. Half its livestock was gone, 40 per cent of its crops destroyed. Its railroads and highways were virtually unusable, and it had a national debt of 176,000,000,000 gold marks — not counting the billions of dollars yet to be demanded as reparations by the allies. Ten times as much currency

was in circulation as in 1914, and it was worth a fraction of what it had been formerly.

These were a few of the facts of German life the newly founded Republic had to face — these, and the growing strength of the revolutionary Spartacists, who had almost succeeded in taking over in the final days of the war.

Founded on the shotgun marriage of militarists with moderate socialists and would-be democrats, the Republic immediately effected further unholy alliances. The "Free Corps," a band of jobless volunteers and professional soldiers, were surreptitiously enlisted to fight off possible revolution. They were not only fanatically anti-Bolshevist, they were anti-democrat, and hopelessly out of sympathy with the Republic they had been engaged to protect. With the tacit approval of the government, they put down the Communists, martyred the Communist leaders, Rosa Luxemburg and Karl Liebknecht, removed the immediate threat of revolution and stayed on. The war was over, but thanks to the "Free Corps" Berlin street fighting in a single week of 1919 claimed 1000 casualties.

The art of political murder, hitherto virtually unknown in Germany, became a popular pastime. With this motley, violent crew of freebooters, vagrants and mercenaries, German democracy saved its skin and mortgaged its soul.

Meanwhile the Constitution of the new Republic was drawn up and signed in Weimar, the home of Goethe and Beethoven. Based on President Wilson's Fourteen Points, asking for simultaneous disarmament of all nations, the prevention of war through compulsory arbitration of international disputes, universal education, a democratic army, special rights for organized labor, freedom of speech, the press, religion, learning and art, it was a noble document — intelligent, benign, informed with hope.

But already the government that it was meant to guide had sold its democratic birthright for temporary safety, and had, by a simple and inevitable act, hopelessly compromised any chance of popularity with the German people. It had signed the Versailles Treaty. In the common mind, this meant that it had accepted "injustice without example." Although no one could have done otherwise, the Republic had betrayed the Fatherland. Furthermore, the foundations it had built upon, Wilson's vision of a brave new world, had already been swept away by Europe's intransigeants and America's irreconcilables. Considering how it levitated — nothing supporting it — and that only a handful really cared much about its survival, it is remarkable that the Weimar Republic didn't dissolve before it jelled.

But it jiggled on, threats of revolution and counterrevolution nibbling continually at its confidence and security. If the "internationals" were put down, the nationalists, even more unfriendly to the spirit of moderation, sprang up. With the specters of starvation and inflation forever at its elbow, there could be no real peace.

In January 1921 one dollar would buy 45 marks; by fall 1922 it would buy 7000. In January 1923, when the French occupied the Ruhr and German heavy industry closed down in protest, the rate jumped from 8000 to 30,000 to 49,000. In July it was 160,000 to the dollar; on October 1st, 242 million; on November 20th, 4 trillion, 200 billion. A single newspaper cost 200 billion marks.

To carry the marks it required larger bags than those for the groceries they bought, although the face of each slip of paper money was covered with zeros. A Communist coup threatened in Saxony and Thuringia, and in Munich Adolf Hitler, a bush-league demagogue, staged his beer-hall *Putsch* and was put away for nine months, long enough to write most of his blueprint for the future: *Mein Kampf*.

The German Republic moved shakily on, losing the allegiance of the ruined middle class and that of many of the workers whose wages had become meaningless, aggravating the contempt of the industrialist profiteers and speculators, the old-guard aristocrats and landowners, who were using the misery of others and the timidity of the government for their own aggrandizement.

Life has become an incomprehensible muddle of numbers [wrote novelist Leo Lania], and no one has the strength left

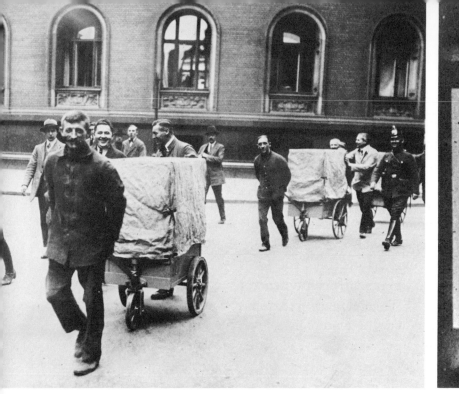

Preis: 1 Billion
100000000000 M
für ein Brot
29. NOV. -23

INFLATION: *Money by the cartload*   *Bread — 1 billion marks a loaf*

to figure out their meaning. And so everyone rushes to cafés, bars, night clubs. Every day a new joint is opened; all the places are overflowing. Since one part of the population has sold everything it possessed and another has exchanged its dollars only for "tangible goods," a clearance sale in human beings has begun. . . . Men who by day profiteer in precious metal or leather trade by night in women and men, love and vice. . . . Secret gambling clubs are set up in the dining rooms of high government officials — the widows of generals rent their bedrooms by the hour — middle-class couples publicly exhibit their sex life for money.

Finally the economic nightmare came to an end. By mortgaging the entire German economy, disallowing war claims, dismissing thousands of public servants, increasing taxes, Stresemann, the chancellor, reversed the inflationary process and, having succeeded in preventing disaster, was promptly forced to resign. The Right and Left, both equally incensed by this last-minute saving of a situation which they had felt could end only in their respective exclusive triumphs, joined forces. Together, they ousted the man who had frustrated them. But they couldn't prevent a feverish prosperity from setting in.

A week's pay

This was 1924, and thus the Weimar Republic's brief "Periclean Age" began. The French withdrew; the war debts were readjusted; national hero Field Marshal Paul von Hindenburg was elected president at seventy-seven and the Locarno Pact reintroduced Germany as a participating member in the community of nations. For four brief years private industry, the states, the municipalities, the churches became the recipients of lavish foreign credit. Improvement and expansion were everywhere. German liners, the *Europa* and the *Bremen,* rivaled in luxury any in the world; German Zeppelins flew higher and farther; German public buildings were more costly and imposing. Unemployment insurance was introduced, covering sixteen million workers.

Adolf Hitler, staging his first Party Day before 20,000 persons in Nuremberg, bewailed the prosperity-begotten "optimism" of the German people. At the opposite extreme, Toller's revolutionaries were complaining of the same good times.

The flimsy structure of the Weimar Republic housed some of the epoch's most exciting thought and art. Artists, writers, scientists snatched their opportunities as if they knew they had only four years to make hay.

In terms of accomplishment and international prestige, Albert Einstein, at the height of his fame, was the Republic's Number

Hindenburg (left)
shooting in Bavais

Grosz

Kandinsky

Einstein (Jo Davidson
extreme right)

The GRAF ZEPPELIN

Kokoschka portrait

Kollwitz

Gropius

UM DEN FISCH by Klee

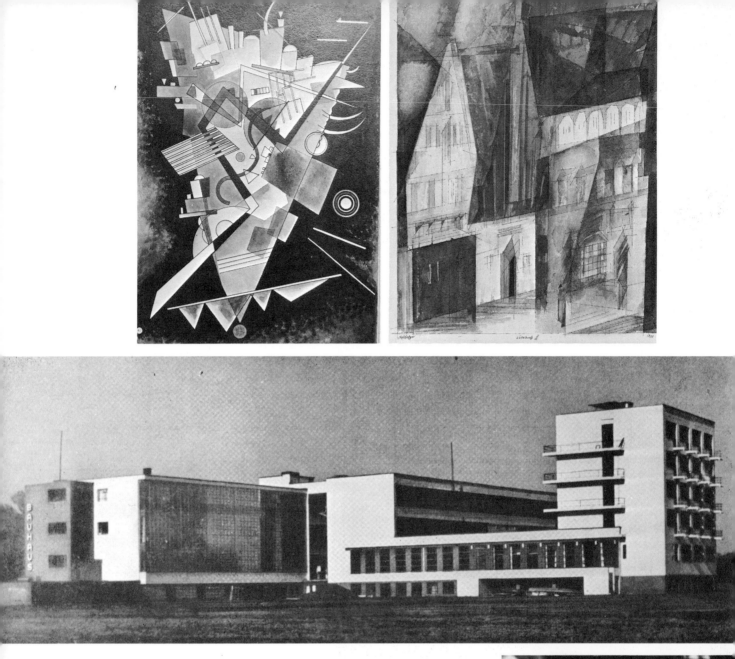

Kurt Weill

The Bauhaus (Dessau)

One citizen. But his residence in Germany was not easy. A humanitarian, a thinker of stunning originality and freedom, and a Jew, he realized he lived among "intolerant, narrow-minded and violent people."

Thomas Mann and his brother Heinrich, half Jews, suffered from a similar apprehension. "The Four Years' War truly looked like the last possible effort of nationalism," wrote Heinrich, "but in running amuck its muscles have not suffered since, and its impetus has grown. It cannot come to a halt until the irrational age has ended, for this was what made it ripe for its deeds; and it lasts and lasts."

Meanwhile Thomas's remarkable *Magic Mountain* was written and Heinrich's depressing and significant *Professor Unruh,* which in time became the frightening movie, *The Blue Angel.*

The same uncertainty and ambivalence seemed to haunt all German art in this brief flowering. The colors of German painting were likely to be lurid, its form and content disquieting. "The verist sets up a mirror in which his contemporaries may see their own grimaces," said George Grosz, whose drawings of German men and women mercilessly reflected the greed, stupidity and arrogance that he saw around him. "I have designed and painted out of a sense of opposition. I have tried in my pictures to show that the present society is ugly, sick, and hypocritical."

The massive canvases of Max Beckmann seemed to substitute power for beauty. Paul Klee, Lyonel Feininger and Vasily Kandinsky — a Swiss, an American and a Russian who chose to live in Germany between the wars — escaped the spirit of the time and place by carefully cultivated subjectivity and abstraction. But an unreal coldness and hysteria never seemed far distant from their work. Even the remarkable institution that gave them shelter, the Bauhaus—which led the world in architecture and design and whose life-span exactly paralled the life-span of the German Republic — was bathed in the same gelid, inhuman light. As if in reaction to the confusion and violence and insecurity around, it must be conspicuously aseptic and calm in its approach to the problems of architecture and design.

German movies (*The Cabinet of Dr. Caligari, The Blue*

Max Reinhardt (center)

Angel, "M") focused on the unpleasant aspects of life with the same cruel clarity as German painting. German drama, like the Toller extravaganza mentioned above, was grim, mannered and bloodless. "The war came and took them and they hated their chiefs and obeyed orders and killed each other," wrote Toller. "And it's all forgotten. They'll be taken again and kill each other. Again and again. That's what people are. They might be different if they wanted to. But they don't want to. They mock at life. They scourge it and spit upon it and crucify life."

German jazz was the tinniest and most insinuating in the world. The serious music Germany introduced tended to be harsh and dissonant and, to all but the initiate, disturbing. A Berlin newspaper critic after the world premiere of Alban Berg's *Wozzeck* wrote in a passion of resentment: "As I was leaving the State Opera, I had the sensation of having been not in a public theater but in an insane asylum. On the stage, in the orchestra, in the stalls — plain madmen. . . . One may ask oneself seriously to what degree music may be a criminal occupation. We deal here, from a musical viewpoint, with a capital offense."

Kurt Weill and Bertold Brecht's *The Threepenny Opera* — according to Hans Hanscheiner "the weightiest possible lowbrow opera for highbrows, and the most full-blooded highbrow musical for lowbrows" — was first produced in Berlin in August, 1928. It marked the peak and term of that city's golden age. Jazzy and dissonant, melodious and sinister, it is unmatched in the abjectness of its cynicism, the haunting potency of its score.

Art grew from life, and life took its cues from art.

German political extremists divorced themselves from all morality. The proof that right and wrong had nothing to do with Right and Left, that there was little choice between radical and reactionary when you got down to cynical essentials, need not have waited till the Spanish Civil War or World War II. It was there, all along, across the Rhine, for anyone to observe who cared to.

The day-to-day living of the German people was as excessive as its politics. The iron discipline of prewar Germany gave way to flamboyant license, which in its turn was replaced by a dis-

cipline more depraved than any abandonment or debauchery possibly could be.

It was decadent — and at the same time undeniably exhilarating from a creative point of view. But it was the exhilaration of the survivors of a traffic accident who sense yet another and more disastrous one impending before they reach home.

The Crash came, hitting the United States and the rest of the world — nowhere with more disastrous results than in Germany. In 1928, American loose money began to stay at home, attracted by the huge interest rates available in a boom economy. Even before October 1929 Germany began to feel the pinch. With the Crash, disaster once more descended and deepened. The German unemployed climbed by millions and unemployment insurance became impracticable and useless. The political situation deteriorated. Some twenty-eight parties struggled for control of the Reichstag; chancellors and elections followed each other with bewildering speed. The Constitution was winked at and the electorate bypassed. Weird coalitions between the Right and Left were formed and dissolved and both political extremes prospered as never before. The membership in the Nazi Party (backed by native and foreign capital, as a bulwark against the Communists) leapt 1000 per cent in a few months. The Communists, larger to begin with, increased their numbers further, by 40 per cent.

At the end of 1930, pro-Hitler students were throwing stink-bombs in protest against Kurt Weill's latest opera *Mahagonny*. Exhibitions of expressionist art were closed in Saxony and Thuringia. There were raids on the homes and stores of Germany's 600,000 Jews. Swastikas and *Juden* appeared on billboards and shop windows. Fighting in the streets returned; in 1931 there were 15,000 casualties.

Like a long train which stops at every dingy little station [wrote English novelist Christopher Isherwood of 1931 in Berlin], the winter dragged slowly past. Each week there were new emergency decrees. . . . The exhausted public had been fed with surprises to the point of indigestion. People said that the

Nazis would be in power by Christmas; but Christmas came and they were not. . . .

Berlin was in a state of civil war. Hate exploded suddenly, without warning, out of nowhere; at street corners, in restaurants, cinemas, dance halls, swimming-baths; at midnight, after breakfast, in the middle of the afternoon. Knives were whipped out, blows were dealt with spiked rings, beer-mugs, chair-legs or leaded clubs; bullets slashed the advertisements on the poster-columns, rebounded from the iron roofs of latrines. In the middle of a crowded street a young man would be attacked, stripped, thrashed and left bleeding on the pavement; in fifteen seconds it was all over and the assailants had disappeared. . . .

And morning after morning, all over the immense, damp, dreary town . . . young men were waking up to another workless empty day. . . .

At the beginning of March, 1932, the posters for the Presidential Election began to appear. Hindenburg's portrait, with an inscription in gothic lettering beneath it, struck a frankly religious note: *He hath kept faith with you; be ye faithful unto Him.* The Nazis managed to evolve a formula which dealt cleverly with this venerable icon and avoided the offense of blasphemy: *Honour Hindenburg; Vote for Hitler.*

Mid-March, eleven million voted for Hitler, the man who hated the Weimar Republic, hated the Jews, hated modern art and modern music, and was backed by some of Germany's biggest landowners and industrialists. In April, in a second election, thirteen million voted for him. He wasn't president, but his bullies now became more brutal. Chancellor Heinrich Bruening, the man who had dared impose a ban on the Storm Troops and Black Guards of the Nazis, resigned — and with his going the last hope of constitutional government in Germany disappeared. The Weimar Republic's time had finally run out. Colonel Franz von Papen, Bruening's successor as chancellor, represented the landholders, the aristocrats, the industrialists who had despised the sickly democracy from the start. To insure his supporters' interests against any liberal or revolutionary intrusion, he attempted to harness the power of the Nazis, and ended by joining forces with Hitler and signing over the Chancellorship to him. It was the last coalition government. In two months a cabinet made up originally of an 8 to 4 majority of non-Nazis was to become 100 per cent Nazi, and the duly appointed Chancellor would be the Dictator of the Third Reich. Hitler's terror began.

In January 1933, just a breath before Hitler unequivocally established his supremacy, Novelist Heinrich Mann wrote an epitaph and an apologia for the Weimar Republic:

> At best, the governments of the Republic behaved like actors on rehearsal, not as if it were evening and the real thing. They only went through the motions of defending and maintaining a state. Logically, they were not around for the play's decisive performance.
>
> For some of the Republic's years, after the revolution and before the civil war, these people knew themselves free, for once, and they will not forget the experience. The people were on the right way; they were halted only by economic distress, which made them listen to the furious rhapsodist of a "Third Reich" while in the Republic they held the practical promise of an even more popular state right in their hands. . . .
>
> Many a man feels called to an inner change after some disaster in his life; but nobody lets him make it, others regard him as what he always was, and he does not seriously believe in his new Adam either. So it went with the Republic of Weimar.

WAILING DAY
ON WALL STREET

IF YOU BISECTED the years between November 1918 and August 1939, the month of division would be March 1929. However, by common consent the real point of division is October of the same year. Americans were allowed a little better than a decade following the Armistice to enjoy the illusions of escape, of getting away with it in uneasy, frantic pleasure. Following that they were given a little less than a decade to sober up, dry out, slip inexorably toward a precipice whose height no one really knew.

The occasion of confrontation, the about-face, the moment of truth, the beginning of the declivity, has since been called *"the Crash."*

Until October 1929, people could delude themselves that peace and the boom were permanent facts of life. It was an article of faith not only for the folk heroes which the manipulators of Wall Street had become, but for the legislators, the Secretary of the Treasury, the President of the Republic himself.

"No Congress of the United States ever assembled, on surveying the state of the Union, has met with a more pleasing prospect than that which appears at the present time," said outgoing President Calvin Coolidge in his Congressional valedictory in December 1928. "In the domestic field there is tranquillity and contentment . . . In the foreign field there is peace, the good will which comes from mutual understanding. . . ."

"Poverty will be banished from the nation," said incoming President Herbert Hoover. "The future of the country . . . is bright with hope."

Tranquillity and contentment were hardly the words. In the domestic field the populace was galvanized by the antics of a bull market which was opening unparalleled vistas of greed, adding new dimensions to the wildest dreams of avarice. Abroad, the prophecies and lamentations of Woodrow Wilson ("utter destruction and contempt") were enjoying ever more sinister confirmation.

The Crash would bring the antics to an end, and hasten the prophecies of doom toward their fulfillment.

Only a small proportion of Americans ever bought and sold on the stock market. Less than a million were estimated to have been involved at the height of the boom, and only a fraction of them took part in the buying-on-margin which represented the bull market at its most sophisticated and precarious. But the plungers had become surrogates for the rest of the population. Every community, every parish, every street seemed to have its citizen who had made a killing. Like rich relations, the speculators were deplored publicly and secretly admired by those timider and less fortunate than themselves. At the end, no one was spared the punishment brought on by the folly of a minority — perhaps because the majority, whatever they may have said, suffered the get-rich-quick fools gladly.

That the ultimate wages of speculative foolishness were financial death had been demonstrated vividly in the immediate past. In the early Twenties Charles Ponzi, a Boston swindler, had built a financial pyramid of the most rudimentary sort by paying off early investors with capital furnished him by a growing horde of victims, eager to share in the spoils. It took eight months for the towering construction to collapse, taking the savings of 40,000 gullible Americans with it.

Ponzi served a brief prison term and then reappeared in Florida, where a land boom, the most flatulent in the history of the Republic, was in progress. "Sparkling sapphire waters caressing glistening white sands," sang the ads, as worthless lots sold for $10,000 in the morning, were sold again (on option) for $20,000 by nightfall. Fortunes on paper were made — and, finally, blown away, along with the glistening white sands, in the big hurricane of 1926.

The lessons were clear, but no one applied them. The stock market was *different*. It had nothing to do with the artful schemes of a single swindler, or of a group of real estate promoters. The stock market regulated the entire economic life of the nation — it expressed it, it was the nation's health and prosperity. Although the Twenties were rife with professional cynics and accomplished debunkers, none had the courage to challenge the health of the bull market. Possibly because they were in it too. There was just one who sniffed a bit. "You give the country four more years of this Unparalleled Prosperity," wrote that perceptive skeptic Will Rogers, "and they will be so tired of having everything they want that it will be a pleasure to get poor again."

It is difficult to say precisely when the first premonition of horrid things-to-come appeared. In 1928 the market broke seriously at least twice. In June, Radio dropped 23 points in a day, and a New York newspaper announced prematurely: "Wall Street's bull market collapsed yesterday with a detonation heard round the world." In December Radio fell 72 points in one day's trading. But over the year, Radio had gone from 85 to 420 and what some might have called a break soon appeared to be a strategic withdrawal to lunge ever farther upward.

Any attempt to moderate the upward surge was rejected. President Hoover voiced disapproval and beached the White House yacht; the Federal Reserve Board tried to introduce an element of caution. Both counsels of discretion were ignored.

"The economic condition of the world seems on the verge of a great forward movement," Bernard Baruch informed his friend Bruce Barton midway through 1929. Brokers' loans were adding four hundred million dollars to their total each month; in three months, in the summer of 1929, industrial averages rose 110 points, more (by nearly a quarter) than in the whole preceding year. J. P. Morgan had ordered a new and bigger yacht and installment buying had reached unprecedented heights. Chrysler had built a 68-story building; the Rockefellers had started a whole city of skyscrapers, and the country club districts of America bristled with phony Italian villas and English manor houses. Black, Starr and Frost had assembled a seven-hundred-thousand-dollar pearl necklace for some lucky woman, and Dusenberg's custom-made automobiles were selling for fifty thousand dollars, limit two to a customer.

According to scholars, the bull market formally came to an end on September 3, 1929. What some optimists preferred to consider a "permanently high plateau" was actually an impenetrable ceiling from which the rocketing stocks could only carom in one direction — down.

Like Krazy Kats on severed branches, it took most of the speculators some time to realize that nothing was holding them up. Their chins permanently tilted to catch the chalk marks on their brokers' boards, they had never registered that employment and production had gradually fallen away beneath them. By Thursday, October 24, they were clawing air. Close to thirteen million shares were sold. The tickers ran hours behind. Tuesday, October 29, was what John Kenneth Galbraith calls "the most devastating day in the history of the New York Stock Market," adding that "it may have been the most devastating day in the history of markets." Those few who hadn't already hit bottom sensed that they might be next.

I have been in Washington on Inauguration Day, Claremore on the Fourth of July, Dearborn on Edison's Day [wrote Will Rogers on October 29, without so much as an I-told-you-so]. But to have been in New York on "Wailing Day"! When Wall Street took that tailspin, you had to stand in line to get a window to jump out of, and speculators were selling space for bodies in the East River.

The great divide of the Years Between had been crossed; the descent began.

THE VOICES

IT IS A TRUISM that from times of desperation and crisis grow both great statesmen and political monsters. For good or ill the challenge is met, and the leadership, to glory or destruction, provided.

At their lowest ebb, the Years Between welcomed the two figures of the era whose acts would doubtless be longest remembered among the commonality of mankind — Franklin Roosevelt and Adolf Hitler. The countries that produced them had boasted no leaders of stature since the First World War dethroned the Kaiser and that same war's aftermath reduced Woodrow Wilson to an embittered and ineffectual old man. Suddenly, early in 1933, within a five-week span, the political vacuums were filled. Thenceforth, Roosevelt and Hitler commanded the attention of their respective countries — of their hemispheres and of the entire world — as no other two men. More and more they became the world's real antagonists, the personification of good as against evil, health as against sickness, reason as against unreason, moderation as against violence.

Although half of their political careers, and the most dramatic half, fell outside the interbellum period, the first hundred days of their power gave the measure and inclination of each man.

The principal instruments of their leadership were their voices, disseminated by radio, repeated and amplified, until, short of deafness, there seemed no escape.

Roosevelt's voice was that of the highly educated product of American privilege, unfailingly upperclass, firm, slightly sibilant and nasal, invested with a unique power of emphasis and the ability to convey a conviction just short of the embarrassment of fervor. Never flowery nor uncomfortably obscure in allusion, his oratory was the reasonable kind, appealing to the emotions of his listeners but not inflaming them, persuasive but not homiletic, friendly and approachable, never cajoling or patronizing for all the "society" twang.

"A second-class intellect," the patriarch Oliver Wendell

Holmes said of him, "but a first-class temperament." The temperament expressed itself in the authority and intuitive aptness of his speech.

Hitler, the Austrian *petit bourgeois*, poor, self-educated, frustrated, snubbed, and finally vindicated in the certainty of his mission, spoke ungrammatical German — harangued, exhorted — in a voice shrill with hysteria. Cracked, strident, imperious, his delivery made no attempt to recommend itself to the listener's ear, nor were his four-hour harangues geared to the normal demands of attention or reason. Repetitive, illogical, incoherent, crafty and insanely candid by turns, his diatribes by some vicious chemistry induced a frenzied response from his German listeners, and disgust and fear from most others.

On March 4, 1933, Franklin Delano Roosevelt was inaugurated as President of the United States. On parade, in top hat and astrakhan-collared greatcoat, he greeted the public with a jaunty wave and a serviceable official smile. On the porch of the Capitol, where he was aided to the stand by his son James, his expression was appropriately earnest, its periodic grimness underlined by the lantern jaw and given a glint by the pince-nez over the small closely spaced eyes creped in deep circles beneath.

"I am certain that my fellow Americans expect that on my induction into the Presidency I will address them with a candor and a decision which the present situation of our Nation impels. This is pre-eminently the time to speak the truth, the whole truth, frankly and boldly."

Thus the voice which was to become so familiar in succeeding years, and more carefully attended to by more constituents than any President's in history, began its first official pronouncement. Edmund Wilson, down to cover the occasion for the *New Republic,* could hear only "the echoes of Woodrow Wilson's eloquence without Wilson's exaltation behind them." Most of his journalistic effort went into a supercilious description of the three-hour inaugural parade. His summation: "There is a suggestion, itself rather vague, of a possible dictatorship."

However, London's *Observer* had a different reaction:

> America has found a man. In him . . . the world must find a leader. Undaunted by the magnitude of his stupendous task and cool in the face of its urgency, Mr. Roosevelt has made a splendid beginning. . . . Calmly and fearlessly he must aim at the highest in international as in domestic affairs. There is no mediocre way for him. His name must be one of the greater names in history or nothing.

Already another leader had put in his bid for immortality, offering his leadership to the people of Germany, and through them to the world. January 30, less than five weeks before the Roosevelt Inaugural, Adolf Hitler accepted the Chancellorship of Germany and began a reign that paralleled almost to the day that of "F.D.R." Sharp-chinned and mustached, with an errant forelock and the uneasy look of a distracted ferret, his words on the occasion of his accession to power were equally memorable:

"More than fourteen years have passed since the unhappy day when the German people, blinded by promises from foes at home and abroad, lost touch with honor and freedom, thereby losing all. Since that day of treachery, the Almighty has withheld His blessing from our people. Dissension and hatred descended upon us. With profound distress millions of the best German men and women from all walks of life have seen the unity of the nation vanishing away. . . ."

In Roosevelt, Wilson's successor had been found and in Hitler the man who would implement Wilson's direst prophecies. Yet, in superficials, the problems that Hitler was facing and the answers he proposed were not unlike Roosevelt's.

"The misery of our people is horrible to behold! Millions of the industrial proletariat are unemployed and starving; the whole of the middle class and the small artisans have been impoverished," said Hitler.

"Values have shrunken to fantastic levels; taxes have risen; our ability to pay has fallen," said Roosevelt. ". . . The withered

Goering and Hitler "for the welfare of Europe and of the whole world"

leaves of industrial enterprise lie on every side; farmers find no markets for their produce; the savings of many years in thousands of families are gone. . . . Only a foolish optimist can deny the dark realities of the moment."

Sixteen million unemployed in America — seven million in Germany. If reporter Wilson saw in Roosevelt's words a vague threat of dictatorship, there were those who saw in Hitler's first speech as Chancellor indications that "he isn't so bad after all," and who thought that giving him the power he had craved might have succeeded in placating him.

Both men certainly expressed a decent concern over the plight of the farmers; both spoke in reassuring terms of the international posture their respective countries might be expected to strike.

Roosevelt's evaluation: "In the field of world policy I would dedicate this Nation to the policy of the good neighbor—the neighbor who resolutely respects himself and, because he does so, respects the rights of others — the neighbor who respects his

St. Louis

Bread in Times Square

Thuringia

obligations and respects the sanctity of his agreements in and with a world of neighbors."

Hitler's: "As regards its foreign policy the National Government considers its highest mission to be the securing of the right to live and the restoration of freedom to our nation. Its determination to bring to an end the chaotic state of affairs in Germany will assist in restoring to the community of nations a State of equal rights. It is impressed with the importance of its duty to use this nation of equal rights as an instrument for the securing and maintenance of that peace which the world requires today more than ever before.

"May the good will of all others assist in the fulfillment of this our earnest wish for the welfare of Europe and of the whole world."

Both struck the spiritual note at the outset and at the end of their perorations:

"So, first of all, let me assert my firm belief that the only thing we have to fear is fear itself," said Roosevelt, echoing the

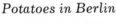

Potatoes in Berlin

New York

Roosevelt in his political prime

wisdom of India's holy men — "nameless, unreasoning, unjustified terror which paralyzes needed efforts to convert retreat into advance. . . ."

"In such a spirit on my part and on yours we face our common difficulties. They concern, thank God, only material things," Roosevelt observed. "The people of the United States have not failed. In their need they have registered a mandate that they want direct, vigorous action. They have asked for discipline and direction under leadership. They have made me the present instrument of their wishes. In the spirit of the gift I take it.

"In this dedication of a Nation we humbly ask the blessing of God. May He protect each and every one of us. May He guide me in the days to come."

"As leaders of the Nation and the National Government we vow to God, to our conscience, and to our people, that we will faithfully and resolutely fulfill the task conferred upon us . . ." said Hitler of the nightmare government he was bringing into power. "It regards Christianity as the foundation of our national morality, and the family as the basis of national life. . . .

"Now, people of Germany, give us four years and then pass judgment upon us. In accordance with Field Marshal von Hindenburg's command we shall begin right now. May God Almighty give our work His blessing, strengthen our purpose, and endow

us with wisdom and the trust of our people, for we are fighting
not for ourselves but for Germany."

Having invoked God's guidance, the two men thereupon
went on their radically different ways.

Throwing himself into his work with a will, Roosevelt opened
Washington to a host of do-gooders, get-it-doners, idealists and
gifted opportunists. After two forbidding chief executives, he
was everybody's friend. His news conferences were breath-
takingly informal. His "Fireside Chats" on radio (the first was
March 12) set a high-water mark for intimacy between political
leader and flock.

Beginning in March, Roosevelt instrumented a score of
measures to improve the country's economy and the lot of its
people: the Emergency Banking Act; the Agricultural Adjust-
ment Act; the Federal Emergency Relief Administration; the
Civilian Conservation Corps; the Public Works Administration;
the Securities Exchange Commission. In May the Tennessee Valley Authority and the Home Owners Loan Corporation were
established, and America went off the gold standard. In June,
the National Recovery Administration began to function, and
the Federal Deposit Insurance Corporation was organized to
protect the savings of the country's "little" man. The little man
also was allowed 3.2 per cent beer and promises of total repeal
of the prohibition amendment.

In this period Franklin Roosevelt sent fifteen messages to Congress [wrote Arthur Schlesinger, Jr.], guided fifteen major laws to enactment, delivered ten speeches, held press conferences and cabinet meetings twice a week, conducted talks with foreign heads of state, sponsored an international conference, made all the major decisions in domestic and foreign policy and never displayed fright or panic and rarely even bad temper.

Roosevelt recalled later, of the final day of his first hundred in office:

> I shall always remember June 16, 1933.
>
> I am certain that this Special Session of the Congress will go down in the history of our country as one which, more than any other, boldly seized the opportunity to right great wrongs, to restore clearer thinking and more honest practices, to carry through its business with practical celerity and to set our feet on the upward path.
>
> I had hoped to get away that night to see my son who was graduating from school and to proceed on a cruise along the New England Coast on a small schooner.
>
> With all letters answered and all work up to date, as far as a President's work can ever be up to date, I left on Friday evening, June 17th, for salt water.

Far from the relaxation of salt water and domesticity, the accomplishments of Hitler in the same period were even more prodigious.

Primary among them were the Reichstag fire, which, on February 27, five days before Roosevelt's Inaugural, gave Hitler the excuse he needed to suspend vast individual and civil liberties throughout Germany. Arrests numbered in the thousands. Newspapers were muzzled; and the election that Hitler desired, to legalize his seizure of power, was assured. It took place one day following Roosevelt's swearing-in, and was the last democratic election Germany as a whole was to enjoy.

A surviving photograph of the Reichstag Fire Trial; defendant is Ernst Torgler

Weimar is dead

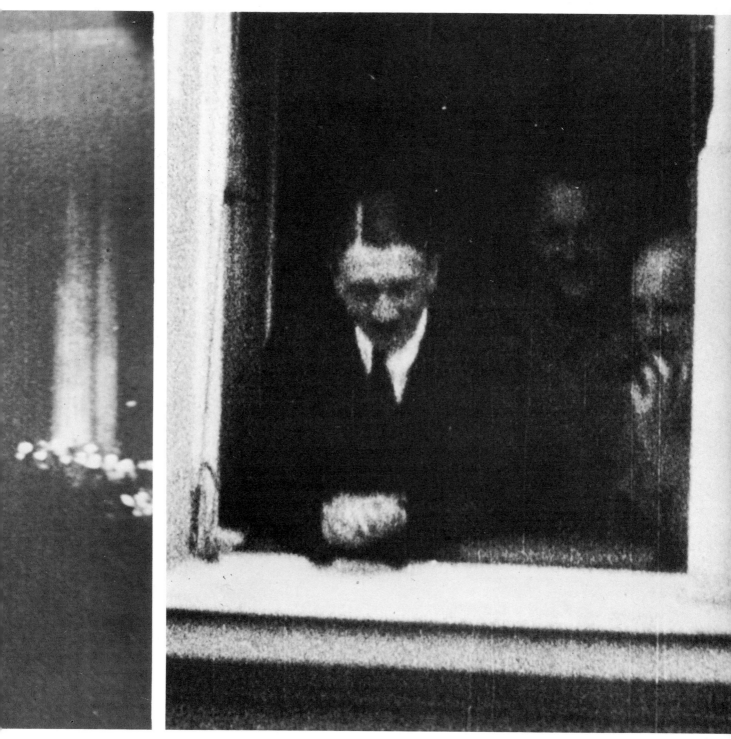

Long live Der Fuehrer

Evidences of Hitler's accomplishments proliferated.

On February 22, on Hitler's instructions, the German Delegation walked out of the Disarmament Conference in Geneva.

On March 11, Carl Ebert, Director of the Berlin Civic Opera, and Fritz Stiedry, its conductor, were dismissed from their posts. On March 15, the broadcasting of Negro jazz was forbidden by Berlin *Rundfunk;* on March 16, a concert in Leipzig was canceled because its conductor, Bruno Walter, was a Jew. On March 21, the Special Court — made up of three judges and no jury — was established to take care of "insidious attacks against the government."

On All Fools' Day, 1933, the new government began its planned campaign of anti-Semitic persecution with the national boycott of Jewish shops and the first Aryan laws. The Gestapo was established and concentration camps opened.

The trek began. It would include the two Manns, Thomas and Heinrich, the two Zweigs, Arnold and Stefan, Einstein, Remarque, Feuchtwanger, among thousands of others. The Bauhaus closed down and the *conférenciers* were stilled. House searchings were instigated and the Reich Defense Council instituted a secret rearmament program.

In May, after addressing an enormous workers' rally with the words "Honor work and respect the worker," Hitler closed all German trade-union headquarters and appropriated their funds; arrested their leaders and dissolved them, outlawing all collective bargaining and strikes.

On May 10 the first book-burning took place on Unter den Linden, opposite the University of Berlin.

That spring, Christopher Isherwood, about to say his final good-by to Berlin, wrote:

> The newspapers are becoming more and more like copies of a school magazine. There is nothing in them but new rules, new punishments and lists of people who have been "kept in." This morning, Goering has invented three fresh varieties of high treason.
>
> Every evening, I sit in the big half-empty artists' café by

the Memorial Church, where the Jews and left-wing intellectuals bend their heads together over the marble tables, speaking in low, scared voices. Many of them know that they will certainly be arrested — if not today, then tomorrow or next week. So they are polite and mild with each other, and raise their hats and enquire after their colleagues' families. Notorious literary tiffs of several years' standings are forgotten.

Almost every evening, the S. A. men come into the café. Sometimes they are only collecting money; everybody is compelled to give something. Sometimes they have come to make an arrest. One evening a Jewish writer, who was present, ran into the telephone box to ring up the police. The Nazis dragged him out, and he was taken away. Nobody moved a finger. You could have heard a pin drop, till they were gone.

By the end of the summer the tendencies were clear and inescapable, and the voices of the two national leaders separated by much more than their rhythm and tone. Held by the fascination of devising plans and making them work, Roosevelt in recommending the National Recovery Administration to the voters was detailed and specific:

"... We have kept our credit good ... we have put three hundred thousand young men into practical and useful work in our forests and to prevent flood and soil erosion. The wages they earn are going in greater part to the support of the nearly one million people who constitute their families.

"It is obvious that if we can greatly increase the purchasing power of the tens of millions of our people who make a livelihood from farming and the distribution of farm crops, we shall greatly increase the consumption of those goods which are turned out by industry."

Hitler had already taken the whole world and the human spirit as his arena. Such details were unimportant. The prophet had supplanted the practical politician.

"A miracle has taken place in Germany," said Der Fuehrer in Nuremberg, after swearing that Germany would never sur-

Hitler at apogee

render the Saar no matter what the outcome of the approaching plebiscite. "The Nationalist Socialist Revolution has overthrown the republic of treason and perjury, and in its place has created once more a Reich of honor, loyalty and decency . . . the overwhelming majority of the German people had already declared itself for our principles . . . The great historian, Mommsen, once characterized the Jews in the life of nations as a 'ferment of decomposition.' In Germany this decomposition had already made great progress. National Socialism opposed with fierce resoluteness this creeping 'decline of the West,' because we were convinced that those inner values which are natural to the civilized nations of Europe, and to our own German nation in particular, had not yet been completely destroyed . . . To save a nation one must think heroically. But the heroic thinker must always be willing to renounce the approval of his contemporaries where truth is at stake.

"The higher race — at first higher in the sense of possessing a greater gift for organization — subjects to itself a lower race and thus constitutes a relationship which now embraces races of unequal value. Thus there results the subjection of a number of people under the will of only a few persons — a subjection based

simply on the right of the stronger, a right which, as we see it in nature, can be regarded as the sole conceivable right because founded on reason. . . .

"Gradually there grew up within the Reich of lamentable absurdity a core of fanatical devotion and ruthless determination. . . ."

Thus spoke the men at the outset of their pilgrimages into history. One was to bring his country out of its worst depression and through its most terrible war, triumphantly. The other was to lead his country into paths of destruction and defeat that would bring it to its lowest physical and spiritual condition in several centuries.

And, as they had come to power within a few weeks of each other, so they died in the same month, April 1945 — Roosevelt just over the threshold of his fourth term as President and on the eve of Germany's total defeat; Hitler, two and a half weeks later, expiring at almost the precise moment that the state he had brought into being was extinguished.

THE PALL

IN THE FIRST MONTH of 1933, the winds began. Cold, hard, from the north, they bore down on Kansas and grew in strength as the days wore on. Dust started drifting back and forth across the fields, digging craters four to five feet deep. Near Dalhart, Texas, by the time Franklin Roosevelt took office on March 4, dunes had formed, making miniature Saharas out of the once fertile fields — and the winds blew on into spring.

The wheat crop was abandoned and the farmers and their families developed a mysterious ailment called "dust fever." In the Oklahoma Panhandle forty destructive windstorms were logged in a few months' time — and it got worse.

On Armistice Day the Southern plains were covered with a frightening pall:

> By noon, it was blacker than night, because one can see through night and this was an opaque black. It was a wall of dirt one's eye could not penetrate, but it could penetrate the eyes, ears and nose. . . . They were afraid, because they had never seen anything like this before. When the wind died and the sun shone forth again, it was a different world. There were no fields, only sand drifting into mounds and eddies that swirled in what was now but an autumn breeze. . . . In the farmyard, fences, machinery, and trees were gone, buried. The roofs of sheds stuck out through drifts deeper than a man is tall.

The next spring a huge wind blew out of the west, raising a cloud of dust — towering three miles high, obscuring the sun from Texas to the Canadian border. It moved eastward at sixty to one hundred miles an hour. By nightfall, Chicago and the Ohio River Valley were under its shadow; two days later it dumped its freight of dust over the entire Eastern seaboard. Dust sifted into the White House, powdering the top of the President's desk, and ships three hundred miles at sea wirelessed to report an inexplicable covering of grit on their open decks.

The topsoil of the United States was blowing away. In one

storm it was estimated three hundred and fifty million tons of it were swept off the wheatlands of the Great Plains and sprinkled over the rest of the nation. Twelve million tons were dumped on metropolitan Chicago alone.

Onto a nation already ground under by the Crash, demoralized by breadlines, bonus armies and bank holidays, had descended the most frightening judgment of all — the richness of the land reduced to dust.

It was like a chapter from the Book of Exodus, only it was difficult to determine who were intended to be the Egyptians, who the Israelites. Was Franklin Roosevelt Pharaoh or Moses? And how could he lead his followers to the promised land when they had thought for so long that they were already in it?

The great dust storms of the Thirties were an even greater shock to the beleaguered "American way of life" than the stock market debacle which preceded them and which had helped to hasten their arrival. For the dust — unlike the painful residue of watered stock, paper profits, bond bubbles — had its origins in the good American earth. The market crash meant the end of an unhealthy illusion; the dust threatened the source of life itself.

Rising up from the last frontier, the place where Americans most recently had confronted nature and assumed victory over it, thunderheads of dust, like huge malevolent genies, crouched over the plains of Texas, Oklahoma, Kansas, New Mexico, Colorado, the Dakotas . . . nature's answer to greed, ignorance, despoliation.

Little more than a half-century earlier, the white men had invaded the grasslands in force. The great herds of buffalo had been slaughtered; iron tracks had been laid, cutting into what had been for centuries inviolate turf. Next came the cattlemen, then the sheepherders and the farmers.

By 1900 the giant plow-up had begun. Topsoil was, according to the Department of Agriculture, the nation's number one inexhaustible resource; for tens of thousands of years, the ever-returning grass had been building a rich loam, layer by imperceptible layer; and in 1900 it was lying there waiting to be turned and seeded. For a few months in 1913 there were premonitions

of what might yet come. But then it was only one county in Kansas that had been turned into a desert of dust, and by June the rains returned. The alarm, the Great Plains reasoned, had been false.

War came, and the failure of European crops. The United States entered with a cry *Win the war with wheat!* In 1917 there were forty-five million acres of United States land in wheat; in 1918, fifty-nine million. By the end of the war twenty-seven million new acres had been planted. The tractors and combines, as big as dinosaurs, crept westward, eating up the Plains.

It was possible for a Plains farmer to plow, seed, cut, thresh, and reseed five hundred acres a year working three months out of twelve. The Wheat Queen of Kansas, Mrs. Ida Watkins, had two thousand acres under cultivation and was adding to them every year. Hickman Price of Plainview, Texas had thirty-four thousand, five hundred acres furrowed and planted.

Chicago policemen, retired schoolteachers, dentists, chiro-

practors — "suitcase farmers" — descended on the Plains, worked a few weeks harvesting one crop and planting another, then went back to their regular jobs. Cattlemen with shrinking ranges increased the number of cattle per acre; and the grass that had not been turned under by the farmer's plow was trampled and torn up by the hungry herds of men greedy for quick returns. It was the Gold Rush all over again — and the claims were running out.

Throughout the Twenties, despite the boom, wheat prices declined but the farmers found that by plowing up more acreage, planting more, buying bigger and better machines, they could keep ahead of the game.

In the 1929 Crash the bottom fell out of the wheat market, but a million more acres of the Texas Panhandle were plowed up. In 1930 the rains stopped falling but not the price of wheat. It dropped to twenty cents a bushel in 1931, less than a tenth of what it had been a dozen years earlier. In 1932 there were violent hailstorms, cutworms, more drought — but even with the resulting shortages the price never went above thirty-five cents the bushel;

and the plow-up to keep one's head above water continued.

"One thing only mattered then—to save our investments somehow. The best way seemed to plow, and plow and plow. . . . It was still a good country — the best damned country a farmer ever saw. Only the price was wrong."

That was 1932. In 1933 the winds began.

As it approached, there was a great rush. . . . Then darkness — total, utter darkness — as it struck. The darkness was dust. The windows turned solid pitch; even flower boxes six inches beyond the pane were shut from view. . . . Dust sifted into the houses, through the cracks around the doors and windows — so thick that even in well-built homes a man in a chair across the room became a blurred outline. It hurt to breathe, but a damp cloth held over mouth and nose helped for a while. As the front of the storm roared on, the people quickly became aware of an awful oppressing silence. They were frightened. More than one, feeling a sudden impulse, fell to his knees and prayed. . . .

The Exodus began — began without a Moses or Aaron. People rose from the table, left the unwashed dishes and the lights burning, and piling into the family jalopy headed west. As they went a great cloud of dust blew across their path. The storm of March 20, 1935, was the worst America had ever known. Five hundred million tons of topsoil went — twice as much in a few hours as that removed by men and machines working seven years to dig the Panama Canal. All of Nebraska's crop went, half of Kansas's and one fourth of Oklahoma's.

Amelia Earhart flew across the great storm's path. "I couldn't see a thing. I don't have the faintest idea what Texas looked like. . . . I was on radio beam most of the way."

As the trek continued it left behind 325 million acres of land destroyed, damaged, threatened.

In Kansas the storms were brown; in Oklahoma red; in Texas and New Mexico, dirty yellow. Dust pneumonia clogged the lungs of those who stayed behind. A gallows humor about it all devel-

oped: about the crows who had learned to fly backwards to keep the dust out of their eyes . . . the pilot who bailed out of his dust-clogged plane only to find it took him six hours to shovel his way back to earth . . . the Oklahoma Panhandle farmer who fainted when a drop of rain struck him in the face and who was revived only by three buckets of sand. In Texas they called dust "Vitamin K."

In the spring of 1935 the wind blew for one hundred hours without stopping, and Plains doctors canceled operations because they could not keep their instruments sterile. Even the tumbleweed died.

From 1935 onward, a million refugees hit the road. It wasn't only the dust. The tractors that had broken the Plains had turned the landowners into tenants, tenants into paupers. Those who hadn't had the land blown out from under them had lost it anyway.

Their Canaan was California, the Northwest. Along Highway 66 — over a rough approximation of the Oregon Trail — through the tableheads of New Mexico, the buttes of Wyoming, the deserts of Arizona, Utah, eastern Oregon, chugged and coughed and shuddered tall square-shouldered cars, piled high with everything that could be tied down.

"I like to think how nice it's gonna be, maybe, in California." [Thus spoke John Steinbeck's Ma Joad in *Grapes of Wrath*, as she was jogging hopefully toward the land of Goshen.] "Never cold. An' fruit ever' place, and people just bein' in the nicest places, little white houses in among the orange trees. I wonder . . . maybe we can get one of them little white houses. An' the little fellas go out an' pick oranges right off the tree. They ain't gonna be able to stand it, they'll get to yellin' so."

In California, Oregon, Washington, right up to the lip of the Pacific Ocean, the "nicest places" had long since been taken — and the next-to-the-nicest, and the ones next to them. The Joads

and their like were shunted into "Little Oklahomas," "Little Arkansases," "Jimtowns," and "Hoovervilles." On abandoned dumps, in swamps and marginal lands, they were allowed to pitch tents of rags, put together lean-tos of pasteboard; and, if lucky, they were given work in nearby fields and orchards where, indeed, there was "fruit ever' place": grapes, peaches, apricots, nectarines in great abundance, to be picked and packed and shipped away as fast and cheaply as possible.

At first they were welcomed with a lopsided grin as the perfect solution to the shortage of low-price, eager labor. These desperate, broken-spirited families would work for very little, almost for nothing: a dollar and a quarter a day would buy a man: fifteen or twenty cents would get a kid. You could sell them

water for five cents a bucket, charge them five dollars a month for the right to erect their own shanty on your property. For a while, the big operators (farming in the promised land was nearly always a big operation) took them on. Then someone asked a frightening question.

"Is it possible to expect that these people — white Americans who will anticipate American standards of living — will be satisfied with the conditions which the agricultural practices of the State of California impose in labor needs?" inquired Mr. A. S. Arnoll of the Los Angeles Chamber of Commerce. "They are American laborers, susceptible to organization, unionization, and, under the depressing circumstances which must result through lack of employment during the winter in the agricultural employ-

ment field, will they not be the finest pabulum for subversive influence?"

The panic was on. Along the California border "bum blockades" went up to keep out so-called "unemployables." Families were shunted from community to community to avoid the growing burden of a dole that was the only answer to mass starvation. Mr. Arnoll's premonitions were richly justified. There were one hundred and eighty strikes in California between 1933 and 1939 involving agricultural field-workers. None of them were successful — but it took a lot of effort to keep them from being so.

Vigilantes were deputized, fiery crosses flared on the hillsides over the shanty towns where the refugees lived crowded together, shacks were burned out, would-be organizers flogged.

"The mongoose of Americanism dragged the cobra of Communism through the good Santa Clara Valley orchards last night," reported the San Jose *News* of a successful raid with truncheons and pipe-lengths on one union headquarters. "A Communist," one farmer told John Steinbeck, "is the guy who wants twenty-five cents an hour when we're paying twenty cents."

Fleeing the vindictiveness of nature the Okies and Arkies and Texies came up dead against the cruelty of man. It was as though the waste and frivolity of the boom years had to be compensated for somehow; as though they had been singled out to be scapegoats, not once but twice.

There were others.

The Crash had divided the Years Between exactly in half. It seemed the first ten years had been set aside mainly for fun and games — the second for suffering and recriminations.

With the government playing an uneasy referee, man was repeatedly challenged by nature and by his fellow man. The dust was followed by a plague of grasshoppers eating their way across the Plains, drifting against fences and barns, breeding, devouring, dying. In 1936 the Merrimack River, and the Connecticut, Hudson, Delaware, Susquehanna, Potomac, Allegheny, went on a rampage; seven hundred thousand people were homeless, paralyzed, their food supply destroyed. In January 1937 the Ohio River overflowed its banks in the worst flood in American history. Nine hundred people died; five hundred thousand were driven from their homes.

The one hundred and eighty agricultural strikes in California were only a small part of the paroxysms now caused by the struggles of labor and capital. Sit-down strikes, walk-outs, lock-outs, thousands of businesses bankrupt, millions unemployed. Reeling under the Crash, weakened by a deepening depression, both workers and management struggled for some new sort of balance, equally determined to get and hold the advantage.

The Committee for Industrial Organization organized coal, organized automobiles, organized steel. On Memorial Day, 1937, outside the struck plant of Republic Steel in Chicago nine men were killed, one hundred men, women and children injured, when the police fired on union sympathizers carrying stones, brickbats and slingshots. In Monroe, Michigan — in Beaver Falls, Pennsylvania — in Youngstown, Ohio and Massillon, Ohio — violence flared.

There were accusations of Communism and counter-accusations of brutality; of subversion and of exploitation. They were all true and they were all exaggerated. For a while, the intoxication of opposites, of black and white, good and bad, right and wrong, deranged the thinking of the country; and then slowly the adversaries began taking one another's measure less self-righteously, less fearfully than before.

Slowly, with the help of a chastened population, the balance of nature also began to reassert itself. Farmers finally admitted that the straight furrows of their fathers, the big plow-up of the boom, were wrong; that the fight against nature begun by their pioneering forebears could only end in a cautious and solicitous truce without a complete triumph for man or an unconditional surrender from the elements. The land was studied with a new respect, broken by Lister plows into contours that would defeat the wind. It was given back to the grass. A great shelter belt of trees from Canada to the Gulf of Mexico was begun. Cattle were taken off the overgrazed land.

In July 1938, as President Roosevelt entered Amarillo,

Texas, on an inspection trip of the dust-ridden Plains, the rains suddenly came. Riding in an open car through the downpour, he laughed and waved back at the cheering, joyous crowds. "I think this little shower we have had is a mighty good omen," he told the delighted Texans.

Gradually the dunes began to recede. The "Dust Bowl" grew steadily smaller; rains and snows watered down the land. The worst was over.

For those who had left the ruined land things got better too. *Grapes of Wrath* by John Steinbeck — denounced in both Oklahoma and California as "a dirty, lying, filthy manuscript" — shocked the country by its picture of what men could do to their fellow humans already brought low by nature. Public hearings led to aid in cash and food and clothing, to improved housing and new hospitals to serve those most miserably destitute.

There would be setbacks and the false solutions of another war, but from the desolation of the Thirties and its cruelty Americans learned some things about living within the borders of their own country and with their own kind, about providence and charity, that, once the war was passed, might be useful to the world.

The Thirties had challenged the myth that America's natural resources were inexhaustible no matter how despoiled. They had demonstrated that compromise not attrition was the best solution for disagreements between men. If the lesson could be remembered, some good might have come from a difficult decade.

THE BRAVE
AND THE FAIR

AT 10 P.M. GREENWICH TIME, December 11, 1936, a tired, beautifully controlled British voice, emanating from the Augusta Tower of Windsor Castle, spoke to a world collected at its radios:

At long last I am able to say a few words of my own.

I have never wanted to withhold anything, but until now it has not been constitutionally possible for me to speak.

A few hours ago I discharged my last duty as King and Emperor . . .

Slightly distorted by the accidents of the atmosphere, the voice went on, gaining strength as it proceeded:

. . . You must believe me when I tell you that I have found it impossible to carry the heavy burden of responsibility and to discharge my duties as King, as I wish to do, without the help and support of the woman I love. . . . The other person most nearly concerned has tried, up to the last, to persuade me to take a different course. . . .

Ever since I was Prince of Wales, and later on when I occupied the Throne, I have been treated with the greatest kindness by all classes wherever I have lived or journeyed through the Empire. . . .

I now quit altogether public affairs, and I lay down my burden. . . .

And now we all have a new King. . . .

God bless you all.

God save the King.

With these final, irrevocable words, uttered in a strong voice filled with emotion, Edward, lately King Edward VIII, for a quarter of a century Prince of Wales and soon to become the Duke of Windsor, put the keystone on one of the most remarkable romances in history.

It was astounding, and at the same time appropriate, that it was the Years Between that contained this love affair. Earlier would certainly have been too soon; later, too late.

Romance in the Years Between had suddenly become everyone's concern: desperate romance, lyrical romance, illicit romance, celluloid romance and tabloid romance — the disposable wedding license and the hiccup marriage, and the built-in, transferable, unrequited passion.

Freud and Marx, the flapper and the sheik, the Boom, the Crash, Riviera sun and Hollywood shadow — all contributed to the romantic confusion. And the press, with its insatiable curiosity about things that formerly were no one's business, with its ability to magnify the trivial and trivialize the magnificent, promoted love to an international obsession.

("*Publicity was part of my heritage,*" wrote the Duke of Windsor, years later, "*and I was never so naïve as to suppose that my romance was a tender shoot to be protected from the prying curiosity of the press. . . . The press creates; the press destroys.*")

The tabloid romance of the Years Between was any affair odd, sensational or sordid enough to catch a bored and cynical editor's interest. Of such, there seemed to be an endless procession:

Ziegfeld beauty Imogene "Bubbles" Wilson and blackface comedian Frank Tinney, whose hopeless attachment led one to dope, the other to madness.

Lovely showgirl Betty Compton and New York's Jazz Age mayor, Jimmy Walker, observed in the town's best clubs and speakeasies, and (when he fled investigation) in the best places along the French Riviera, until marriage made the lovers less interesting.

Nan Britton, who claimed to have carried illicit romance within the very portals of the White House, where, for purposes

Investiture of the Prince of Wales,
Carnarvon Castle, 1911

of making love, she said she met President Warren Gamaliel Harding in a cloakroom.

Gray-haired Daddy Browning and his fourteen-year-old "Peaches."

Mrs. Ruth Snyder and Henry Judd Gray, a Long Island housewife and a corset salesman who dispatched Mr. Snyder with a window weight, some chloroform and a loop of picture wire for love and a fifty-thousand-dollar insurance policy.

The Reverend Mr. Edward Wheeler Hall and church soloist Mrs. Eleanor Mills, found shot to death among the scattered pages of their torrid correspondence under a crab-apple tree in rural New Jersey.

All the singers of sad songs whose love life was sadder still: Helen Morgan, Fannie Brice, Ruth Etting, Libby Holman:

> AND LET HER LOVES, WHEN SHE IS DEAD,
>
> WRITE THIS ABOVE HER BONES:
>
> NO MORE SHE LIVES TO GIVE US BREAD
>
> WHO ASKED HER ONLY STONES.

These lines by Dorothy Parker could serve as epitaph for the scores of romances in the Years Between that without the vigilance of the press need never have concerned anyone other than their own unfortunate participants.

The affair of the King and Mrs. Simpson was the apotheosis of the news weekly, Sunday supplement, tabloid romance. The Fourth Estate pursued it with an unprecedented gullibility and greed for detail, a bug-eyed attention that finally was fully justified. And the pursuit began, and reached its height, in the magazine of a man not much younger than the King and but recently involved in his own great romance: Henry Robinson Luce.

"While the outcome, no doubt, will be a victory for the throne," quoted *Time* Magazine, October 5, 1936, "the King quite evidently is the most helpless of creatures, a man over forty who has fallen desperately in love."

Mr. Simpson

Wallis Warfield . . . resolved early to make men her career and in forty years reached the top — or almost [said *Time*, January 4, 1937]. Mrs. Simpson from the moment King George V died, began to "help" infatuated King Edward VIII, according to her lights. She helped him to spend thousands of guineas royally, imperially, wildly; and she helped him to pinch pennies, convincing His Majesty that in housekeeping she is most economical. Together they cruised the Balkans in one of the world's costliest yachts, they ransacked Cartier's in Paris for diadems, in October, they picked out ermine skins recently made up in London for Mrs. Simpson's Christmas. . . .

The tone was critical and suspicious — and with some reason.

The romance of the Years Between and of the century had its first stirrings in the unpromising company of the "international set." This loosely knit collection of the noble, the rich and the famous was referred to by one member of the British Old Guard as "that raffish group that now lords it over London society, that mongrel pack of (mainly) immigrant aliens, naturalized or otherwise, the Invaders, the most heartless and dissolute of the pleasure-loving ultra-rich, the hardest and most hated people in England."

This new young Monarch was different [wrote the Duke of Windsor of himself]. While he worked overtime insofar as his duties were concerned, August would probably find him playing golf at Biarritz or swimming off Eden Roc, or stooking wheat on his ranch in Canada. He had abandoned fox hunting for the less virile pursuit of gardening. . . . His free evenings were most likely to be spent "en petit comité" with a few intimates or at the Embassy Club than in the great houses or salons of London.

"He had a craving for private happiness," said the Archbishop of Canterbury. "Let the odd circle which got him away from us stand rebuked by the nation."

This odd circle was obviously poison to some, catnip to others. Cole and Linda Porter thrived on its companionship in Paris, on the Riviera and the Lido. Hollywood queens Gloria Swanson, Pola Negri, Constance Bennett chose mates from its titled cast of characters and quickly returned them. So did the Astors and Vanderbilts, Goulds and Emerys, Barbara Hutton and Doris Duke.

For all its interminable pedigrees and vast bank accounts, its roots were shallow, its attachments weak. Its attitude toward love was casual, its attitude toward marriage cynical in the extreme. Its specialty was not the grand passion or the rich relationship cultivated over the years, but the amusing affair, the convenient marriage.

By virtue of his birth, his charm, his fondness for a good

time, the Prince of Wales stood in its first rank. At the beginning,
Mrs. Wallis Warfield Simpson — neither wealthy nor titled nor
famous — scarcely merited mention among its lowliest and most
recent recruits.

The circumstances of the meeting of the Prince of Wales and
Mrs. Simpson are the subject of some contradiction. The lady
remembered it as having occurred one year, 1930; His Royal High-
ness the next. They both recollected that it took place on a country week end; but friends who claimed to have been present put
it at a gathering in town. There is general agreement, however,
that it was Thelma, Lady Furness — a member in good standing of the international set because of her American birth, English
title, and close friendship with the Prince — who had brought it
about. For some reason an atmosphere heretofore discouraging to

any kind of serious romance breathed kindly on this meeting of a married woman of no importance and the indulged heir to Christendom's greatest throne.

Perhaps the most remarkable thing about the meeting was that it occurred at all.

At the moment of his birth on June 23, 1894, Prince Edward Albert Christian George Andrew Patrick David became the single most important baby alive. His great-grandmother, Queen Victoria, occupied the loftiest throne on the globe and represented in her person the single greatest national power the world had ever produced. Nothing but his own premature death seemed likely to prevent this beautiful baby from assuming that power which, being the eldest son of the eldest son of the eldest son of the Queen, descended directly upon him.

Time converted the beautiful baby into a charming golden-haired boy, then a handsome youth, as it brought him closer to the throne.

In 1901 his great-grandmother died — "a divinity of whom even her own family stood in awe." Dressed in "white tulle cap, black satin dresses, and shiny black shoes with elastic sides,"

A Prince at war

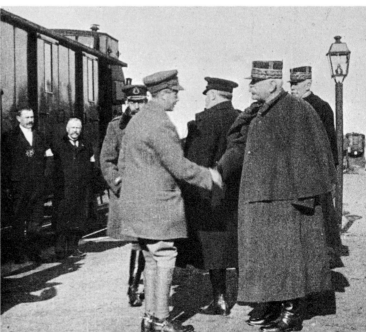

young David remembered her as always being surrounded by a "galaxy of Emperors, Kings, Princes, Grand Dukes and Dukes" — mostly her relatives or descendants.

In 1910 her successor, the Prince's vital, lusty grandfather, Edward VII, died. "In my gallery of childhood memories the portrait of my grandfather seems bathed in perpetual sunlight. . . . Light opera, cards, and a keen interest in the turf," as well as insuppressible gallantry toward pretty women, characterized this formidable figure of a man. Nine monarchs on horseback rode in his funeral cortege.

The following year, within "the vast grey ruin of Carnarvon Castle," his father, George V, invested the seventeen-year-old youth as Prince of Wales, handing over to him the coronet cap, the gold verge of government, the gold ring of responsibility.

"A most charming, unassuming young man, such as one would expect from such a family — but a young eagle, likely to play a big part in European affairs because he is far from being a pacifist," said the Prince's cousin Willy, Kaiser Wilhelm of Germany.

The next summer the royal cousins were at war. "In those four years I mixed with men — in those four years I found my

manhood." The Prince of Wales emerged from the war the world's most conspicuous, most eligible and possibly most dissatisfied bachelor. "There was always something lacking, something not supplied. Given my character, my roving curiosity and independence, my life appeared to form a disconnected pattern — duty without decision, service without responsibility, pomp without power."

His manner of dress became casual and much copied — the Windsor knot, the boater, the backless evening waistcoat, the burgundy boutonniere. He liked fast speedboats, the hazards of polo and the steeplechase. He liked to tap-dance, play the bagpipes, strum a ukulele, go night-clubbing and yachting. Prince Charming, Galahad, Prince of Mayfair, the Salesman of the Empire — these were some of the titles conferred upon him as he circled the globe alternating official functions with race meets, parties, sports, pub-crawling.

Approbation was not universal. "He managed by his choice of friends and diversions, to provoke an exhibition of social climbing on the part of a few Americans which has added nothing to his prestige," wrote one New York newspaper on the occasion of his second visit. In India Gandhi burned his "foreign" clothes to protest the Prince's presence; in Allahabad the Prince drove through empty, silent streets. In London he was criticized for preferring Americans and nouveaux riches to the old-line aristocracy. It was admitted, however, that princes before him had pursued pleasure in the company of questionable friends until responsibility or the love of a good woman set them on the proper path.

Bessie Wallis Warfield, the daughter of a Baltimore clerk of good family but small means, was born at a resort hotel at Blue Ridge Summit, Pennsylvania, in June 1896, just two years after

A Prince at peace

the Empire celebrated the birth of its new prince. Raised in genteel poverty (her father died when she was an infant) she managed, nevertheless, thanks to a rich uncle, a fashionable aunt and an attentive grandmother, to have a proper upbringing and proper friends. The war swept her into a proper marriage, to a young naval flyer from the Middle West.

At this juncture — although the young Prince appeared at a dance at a California hotel where she and her husband were staying (the same Hotel del Coronado where the Sennett Bathing Beauties frolicked and the Boston Brahmins rocked) — his orbit was astrally remote from her own.

In 1928, a second marriage to a well-to-do Anglo-American, Ernest Simpson, brought her to London and eventually to the attention of the playmates of the Prince.

"Wallis Simpson was 'fun.' . . . She was not beautiful; in fact she was not even pretty. But she had a distinct charm and a sharp sense of humor," said Thelma, Lady Furness, her entrée into the Prince's circle. "Her dark hair was parted in the middle. Her eyes, alert and eloquent, were her best feature. Her hands were large; they did not move gracefully and I thought she used them too much when she attempted to emphasize a point." She also served good food, had good taste in clothes and furniture. She would do.

Of their first encounter the Prince recalls a mocking look in Mrs. Simpson's eyes, a cold in her nose and a rather astringent interchange concerning central heating.

Mrs. Simpson was struck by "a strange, wistful, almost sad look about the eyes when his expression was in repose," and judged "the Prince an altogether charming and remote figure, not quite of the workaday world — a figure whose opportunities and behaviour were regulated by laws different from those to which the rest of us responded. I had already dismissed from mind the possibility of our ever meeting him again."

But Lady Furness, as if anxious to find her own successor as the Prince's favorite American, persisted. Wallis was presented at court in finery borrowed from Thelma and her sister. Mr. and Mrs. Simpson were invited to the Prince's country retreat, Fort

Belvedere in Windsor Great Park, where Lady Furness acted as unofficial hostess. There were invitations to cocktails, to dinner at the Simpsons' elegantly simple London flat. There was, eventually, an invitation to Biarritz that Mr. Simpson couldn't accept but Mrs. Simpson could, and a trip aboard Lord Moyne's yacht, the *Rosaura,* along the Spanish and Portuguese coasts.

Often the Prince and I found ourselves sitting alone on deck, enjoying the soft evening air, and that unspoken but shared feeling of closeness generated by the immensity of the sea and the sky. Perhaps it was during these evenings off the Spanish coast that we crossed the line that marks the indefinable boundary between friendship and love. Perhaps it was one evening strolling on the beach at Formentor in Majorca. How can a woman really know? How can she ever really tell?

Then came Cannes, the Italian Lakes; the first jewel — a diamond and emerald dangle for her bracelet. That winter there was skiing at Kitzbühel in the Austrian Alps, and waltzing in Vienna, and on to Budapest for the Gypsy violins and the czardas.

Paper says the Prince of Wales danced with a Baltimore woman in a "multicolored dress of spun glass, and just a single diamond in her hair"! [Will Rogers observed in Beverly Hills.] If that made international news, what would it have been if he had dropped her in that glass dress? Someday there is going to be a society gal that dident dance with him, then you going to hear of real fame.

The next summer it was Cannes and the Duke of Westminster's yacht *Cutty Sark,* and again Vienna and Budapest.

"The core of our marriage had dissolved," Wallis observed later of Mr. Simpson. "Only the shell remained — a façade to show the outer world." The outer world in the know replied with a callous remark about "The Unimportance of Being Ernest."

January 20, 1936, King George V died. The Prince, commented his inamorata, "had become the prisoner of his heritage."

At this moment the royal precedents were obvious; the counsels of the international set, the examples of celluloid and tabloid romance, crystal clear. They all agreed. Had the pattern been followed the Years Between would not have known its most remarkable romance, and England would have known better one of its briefest reigning kings.

It became increasingly plain to me . . . that however wholeheartedly I might adapt myself to the familiar outward pattern of kingship . . . I could never expect wholly to satisfy the expectations of those for whom the rigid modes of my father's era had come to exemplify the only admissible standard for a King. . . . The fault lay not in my stars but in my genes.

In August there was another yacht, Lady Yule's $1,350,000 *Nahlin*. A congenial party was formed — including Mrs. Simpson, three thousand golf balls to drive into the blue Adriatic, and a large stock of champagne. The cruise began down the ancient coast of Dalmatia. But although the manners of the playboy Prince persisted, and the customs of the international set prevailed, there was a difference. There was a King on board.

Behind them they left the preliminaries of Mrs. Simpson's divorce and the first omnious rumbling of the world-wide publicity which would force their romance into the open and drive them into exile. There were other more serious concerns. France must be avoided, since the Popular Front of Léon Blum threatened civil turmoil and Communist flags flew within view of Maxine Elliott's marmoreal Villa l'Horizon at Cannes. Italy must be avoided, because Ethiopia had just been overrun. Spain a month past had begun its bloody civil war. In Vienna there had been assassinations and massacres.

For the moment, however, there were excursions ashore for picnics in deserted coves, the King "in espadrilles . . . little shorts and a tiny blue-and-white singlet" — or, to the scandal of some onlookers, no singlet at all. Peasants threw flowers, danced

in the streets, organized torchlight parades that turned mountains into pyramids of flame in their honor.

But the lighthearted international romance soon began to collide with the monarch's international cares. Casual encounters took on sinister meanings: Prince Paul of Yugoslavia was reported to be pro-Hitler, Admiral Horthy of Bulgaria was rumored the same; Kemal Ataturk might leap either way; King George of Greece was only recently re-established on his precarious throne, and might not be there long. . . . A pleasure cruise became an obstacle course with the whole world watching; and waiting at the end was an unclearable wall.

Back in the British Isles, the Scottish pipers were reported to have played "The St. Louis Blues" at Balmoral for the King's American friends. One million dollars in jewels and fifty thousand dollars' worth of silver foxes were allegedly showered on the King's ladylove. He had ordered the immediate construction of "the world's finest yacht," with swimming pool, squash court, gymnasium, and equipment permitting the King to arrive or depart from his floating palace by seaplane. Hungary's most famous Gypsy bandmaster was en route to play for His Majesty's dinner guests at Buckingham Palace. A London florist revealed that the King was sending Mrs. Simpson twenty-five dollars' worth of long-stemmed red roses per day: fifteen dozen in summer when they were cheap, five dozen in winter when they were dear.

The *chichi* seemed to continue on a scale heretofore unparalleled in the brief and opulent history of international society. But behind the glitter, grim history ground on and a tenacious romance held fast.

Mrs. Simpson got her divorce on the twenty-seventh of October, at the Ipswich Assizes, after a nineteen-minute hearing.

Down with the American harlot appeared chalked on the pavements of Aberdeen. Rents doubled in fashionable Cumberland Terrace, where Mrs. Simpson took up residence; then her house was stoned and every window broken. Her mail contained notes threatening her life: *Beware, the fate of all kings' mistresses will soon be yours.*

Finally, the British press, which had maintained a heroic self-imposed silence, could contain itself no longer.

Mrs. Simpson fled the country, zigzagged down France with the Fourth Estate in hot pursuit, and found shelter with friends on the Riviera.

"It is not because Mrs. Simpson is an American that England would spurn her as a Queen," wrote Hugh Walpole. "It is because the Crown, that very sensitive and vulnerable ideal, would lose caste by union with a woman twice divorced."

Forced by the Prime Minister, the Archbishop of Canterbury, Parliament, the hidebound aristocracy, the Dominions, to make the choice of marriage to Mrs. Simpson or the Throne — prevented from taking his case to the people — the King abdicated.

I reject the notion put forward by some that, faced with a choice between love and duty, I chose love. I certainly married because I chose the path of love. But I abdicated because I chose the path of duty. I did not value the Crown so lightly that I gave it away hastily. I valued it so deeply that I surrendered it, rather than risk any impairment of its prestige. . . .

Watching the shore of England recede, I was swept by many emotions. If it had been hard to give up the Throne, it had been even harder to give up Great Britain. I knew now that I was irretrievably on my own. The drawbridges were going up behind me. But of one thing I was certain: so far as I was concerned, love had triumphed over the exigencies of politics.

For David, now Duke of Windsor, there was a six months' wait in Austria until his intended wife's divorce became final. Then, on June 3, 1937, he made Bessie Wallis Warfield Spencer Simpson, the woman who would have been queen, his first duchess, and, by special designation of the Crown, the last duchess in the land. The wedding dress of "Wallis blue" was by Mainbocher, her hat by Reboux. The ceremony took place in a château borrowed from an international millionaire who died in a Miami

"It was done . . .

a lifetime to regret or rejoice"

jail a few years later awaiting trial as a Nazi collaborator. It was performed by a clergyman forbidden by the Bishop of Durham to solemnize the marriage. None of the Royal Family, to maintain whose prestige King Edward had given up his throne, attended.

It was done, and the Duke and Duchess had a lifetime to regret or rejoice in their decision.

They were scolded: "It is incomprehensible that a man forty-two years old," said Elsa, "who had been trained from infancy to uphold the tradition he inherited, had absolutely no concept of his subjects' reverence for the crown or its symbolic significance.... Edward simply did not have the strength of character or the *noblesse oblige* of King George VI and Queen Elizabeth."

They were applauded: "Everybody needs being excited by the story of Mrs. Simpson at least once a year," said Gertrude Stein:

> ... it cheered up the gloom of organization, and the difference between sovietism and fascism and new deals and sit down striking ... a funny American ... who taught a great many people painting ... used to say remember every room has its gloom and the great thing to do is to find the colour that will cut that gloom. Well organization has its gloom and the only thing for a long time that really cut that gloom was Mrs. Simpson and King Edward and the abdication.

Most eloquent of all, as usual, was Winston Churchill, espouser of unpopular causes, who had been King Edward's champion till the end. "In this Prince there were discerned qualities of courage, of simplicity, of sympathy and, above all, of sincerity," Churchill told Parliament at the time of the abdication. "Qualities rare and precious which might have made his Reign glorious in the annals of this ancient Monarchy. It is the acme of tragedy that these very virtues should, in the private sphere, have led only to this melancholy and bitter conclusion. But although today our hopes are withered, still I will assert that his personality will not go down uncherished in future ages."

Nor, for that matter, hers.

THE LITMUS WAR

THE YEARS BETWEEN, although their very name might imply a recess from violence, could not boast even a momentary calm. Each hemisphere had its military excursions, its rebellions and invasions, police actions and suppressions by force of arms. Abyssinia, Austria and Armenia, Guatemala, Bolivia, Paraguay, Mexico, Germany and Italy were bloody echoes of one great conflict, and rumbling premonitions of another on its way.

China, from 1927 on, was in the grip of a civil war between the Communists and Chiang Kai-shek's Kuomintang, a conflict that still continues at this writing. In 1931 the Japanese invaded Manchuria, thus instigating an undeclared war which nibbled away implacably at China's outlying territories, and in 1937, still undeclared, struck at its heart in Shanghai and Nanking. In less than six months 300,000 Chinese soldiers and 300,000 civilians died. The Chinese Government withdrew to Hankow, and by the end of 1938 was holed up far in the interior in the city of Chungking, leaving over half the country and all the coastal areas in Japanese hands.

However, even the complex disturbances in China, claimed by some as the beginning of World War II, failed to engage the common attention as a blow in the gut might, or a pang around the heart, or a sudden smoke in the brain, but rather as a headline, or the voice of a radio announcer cracked and muted by distance. Except for those immediately involved, or those habitually interested in others' catastrophes — journalists and humanitarians and statesmen — these local wars seemed a matter of curiosity more than concern: other people's business, to be ignored, or, if noted, intentionally forgotten.

And yet in 1936, when a group of professional soldiers rose against the floundering Republican government of Spain, other people's business suddenly became everyone's; curiosity metamorphosed into more than concern — into anger and alarm — into declarations of sympathy and allegiance — into personal action.

The Spanish Civil War roused a world apparently indifferent to bloodletting and bullying. The capacity for indignation re-

Civil disorder . . .

turned, although its righteousness was open to dispute. There were two ways to view the unpleasantness in Spain.

General Francisco Franco, aided by other reactionary militarists, the Fascist Falange, the monarchists, the rich aristocracy and the big landlords . . . launched an insurrection against the liberal, enlightened, legally elected government, according to one interpretation.

Peace, order and justice were languishing, claimed Franco's partisans. *The Church and State must be protected from that Red Flag which is the symbol of the destruction of Spain's past and her ideals.*

Name-calling to divert attention from the real motives characterized both sides.

The moderates, the men of modesty, the good-willed bumblers and not-good-enoughs once again were crushed between the violent and the extreme.

The immediate prelude to war was appropriately ominous. In four months' time (the last four of the Republic), the "liberal, enlightened, legally elected government" saw 160 churches burned to the ground, 269 murders and 1287 bodily assaults attributable to political causes; 10 newspaper offices had been ransacked, 69 party clubs and centers wrecked. There had been 113 general strikes and 228 partial work-stoppages.

The Falangists — the party of the extreme Right — rode round in motor cars mounting machine guns. They committed arson and murder, for the most part undeterred.

On May Day huge posters of Stalin and Lenin marched down Madrid's elegant Castellana followed by Spanish youths giving the clenched-fist salute and singing the Internationale.

The Monarchists had already sent emissaries to Fascist Italy and to Germany, plotting the overthrow of the government which was permitting these things to take place in Catholic Spain.

"We want a revolution; but it is not the Russian Revolution which can serve us as a model," said a Socialist woman deputy in the Cortes, "since we must have huge flames which can be

. . . sacrilege

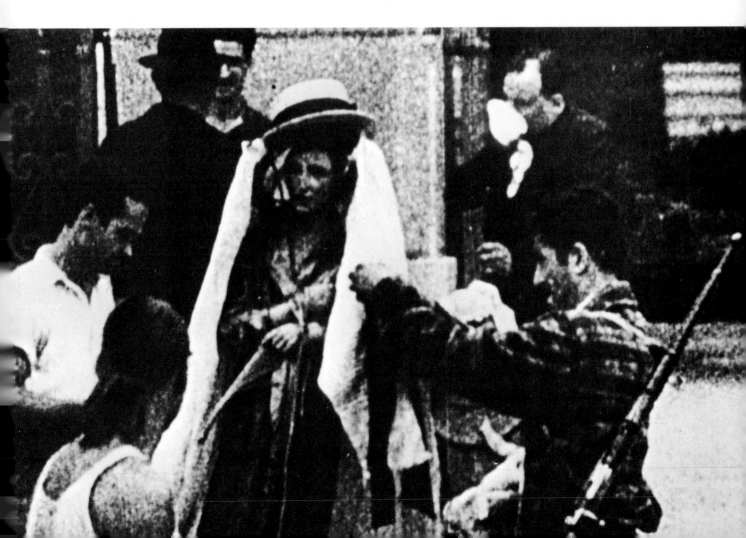

seen all over the world and waves of blood which turn the seas red."

A Communist officer in the Republican *Asaltos* (Shock Troops), Lieutenant José Castillo, was shot down by four armed men on his own doorstep. An assassin himself, Castillo had committed an earlier crime, based on a crime based on a crime based on a crime — an endless boomerang of blood and revenge that mirrored Spain's immemorial pattern.

Later that same night, Calvo Sotelo, the leader of the Monarchists, was arrested under false pretenses, driven into the suburbs and shot in the back of the head.

The two funerals took place in the same cemetery on the same day: July 14, 1936. Three days later, by prearrangement, the long-planned coup began.

Garrisons of Spanish and Moroccan soldiers along the North African coast — Melilla, Tetuan, Ceuta, Larache — rose, and the mutineers assumed the government of Spanish Morocco. On the

The rebels

Spanish mainland Avila, Segovia, Saragossa, Pamplona, Burgos, Oviedo, Cadiz, Cordoba, Teruel quickly fell to similar uprisings.

After a fatal period of hesitation, the Republic consented to the arming of the trade-unions. The insurgents — the Moroccan troops, led by Franco, the mutinous soldiers and their aristocratic allies — now found their principal opposition in the workers. The lines of hostility were drawn, or appeared to be.

In Seville, where General Guelfo de Llano, a career officer, a lush and ladies' man, seized the city in the rebels' name virtually single-handed, the workers were reported massacred to the number of 9000 in a few days' time. In eighteen months 150,000 Andalusians suspected of loyalty to the Republic were estimated put to death, while the general's sodden harangues over Radio Seville promoted chuckles and scandal across the land.

The armed workers and Loyalist troops were no less busy. In under two months they were said to have executed 75,000 of their countrymen.

Brother set upon brother, friend on friend, neighbor on neighbor. In Ronda, one of the most beautiful cities of all Spain, the bourgeoisie were routed out, beaten with flails and driven over the cliff which afforded the town its spectacular site. In

Badajoz the human victims were herded into the bull ring and shot. If Republicans were reported to employ medieval tortures on their victims, their partisans were, in their turn, dispatched with equal brutality by the Insurgents. The pregnant wife of a Republican governor was subjected to an abortion, then thrown living into a grave and shot; the mother of two priests was killed by stuffing a crucifix down her throat. Somewhere between the two warring factions, the great poet García Lorca, seeking a neutral spot where a Catholic with a Socialist brother-in-law might find safety, disappeared from view and was claimed a martyr by a cause he never espoused.

Allegiance to a party or a cause was not required. Birth, class and vocation, blood relationship and relationship by marriage were adequate reasons for assassination by either side.

"It is better to die on your feet than to live on your knees!" shouted La Pasionaria, the hollow-eyed queen of the Spanish Communists, over Radio Madrid. *"No pasarán!"* Unsmiling, dressed always in the black of a peasant woman in mourning, she was said to have slit the throat of a priest with her own teeth.

"Long live Death! Down with Intelligence!" shouted the rebels, adopting also the mindless cry of the Spanish Foreign Legion:

SPAIN — UNITED! SPAIN — GREAT!
SPAIN — FREE! SPAIN — ARISE!

The Republic's struggle against Fascism in Spain was probably the zenith of political idealism in the first half of the twentieth century . . . Bolshevism inspired vehement passions in its foreign adherents but little of the tenderness and intimacy which Loyalist Spain evoked. The Pro-Loyalists loved the Spanish people and participated painfully in their ordeal by bullet, bomb, and hunger. . . . Only those who lived with Spain through the thirty-three tragic months from July, 1936, to March, 1939, can fully understand the joy of victory and the more frequent pang of defeat which the ups and downs of the Civil War brought to its millions of distant participants.

These were the words of Louis Fischer, the first American volunteer in the International Brigade, gone to fight alongside the Spanish Republican Armies. He was joined by thousands more non-Spaniards, impelled toward Spain by a desperate desire to align themselves with the fight for right — Pole, British, French, Hungarian, Belgian, Yugoslav.

Where the world had stood by and let the "liberal, enlightened, legally elected government" of Italy, and then thirteeen years later that of Germany, totter and fall with scarcely a flicker of concern, three years later, in Spain, everyone seemed inclined to take part or at least express his opinion.

> YESTERDAY THE BELIEF IN THE ABSOLUTE VALUE OF GREEK;
> THE FALL OF THE CURTAIN UPON THE DEATH OF A HERO;
> YESTERDAY THE PRAYER TO THE SUNSET,
> AND THE ADORATION OF MADMEN. BUT TODAY THE STRUGGLE.

wrote poet W. H. Auden passionately from England.

It seemed to many, like Auden, that the Spanish War held the vindication of the past and the key to the future. That here good and evil, black and white, retrogression and advance, arranged themselves in neatly opposed ranks; that allegiance could be clear-cut and just, and the enemy silhouetted against the sharply etched Spanish landscape could be picked off one by one.

But Spain was all things to all men, and there were others who were more cynical.

To Mussolini, Spain was just one more means of perpetuating his own glory and keeping the Italians he despised occupied away from home. A "kick in the shin," to keep them up to the mark. According to a bill presented to Franco at a later date, he sent 763 planes, 1411 motors, 1672 tons of bombs, 9,250,000 rounds of ammunition, 1930 cannon, 240,747 small arms, 7,514,537 artil-

The loyalists

Help   from Italy,

from Germany

lery shells, 324,900,000 rounds of small arms ammunition and 7663 motor vehicles. Figures for Italian warships engaged in the Spanish war were 91, besides 92 Italian cargo vessels, with Italian submarines claiming 72,800 tons of hostile shipping sunk.

Account rendered: 7,500,000,000 lire.

After a decent delay, Franco sent five billion.

Germany more systematically and even more cynically used Spain to test its planes and personnel. "I urged him to give support under all circumstances" said Goering of his recommendations to the Fuehrer, who, all things being equal, would have preferred to see the discomfiture of his old enemy, the Catholic Church, rather than support its champions. Goering's motives: "firstly, to prevent the further spread of Communism; secondly, to test my young Luftwaffe in this or that technical respect." Another reason admitted by Hitler was "to distract the attention of the Western powers to Spain, and so enable German rearmament to continue unobserved."

Operation MAGIC FIRE, Germany's code name for their participation in Spain's war, was instituted — with cargo planes, cargo ships and fighters going out on a clockwork schedule. The Condor Legion was formed; German pilots were put at Franco's disposal.

Russia earmarked a thousand million francs to aid the Loyalist government, apparently on the condition that revolution or any appearance of revolution within the Loyalist fold be repressed. This didn't mean that Russians didn't connive to twist events to their ends with growing effectiveness. Eventually, Russian tanks and planes arrived and Russian soldiers and their collaborators assumed high position in the Loyalist ranks.

Never [according to Robert Graves and Alan Hodges] since the French Revolution had there been a foreign question that so divided intelligent British opinion as this. It could be seen in so many ways; as Fascism versus Communism, or Totalitarianism versus Democracy, or Italy and Germany versus England

and France, or Force versus Liberty, or Rebels versus Constitutional Government, or Barbarism versus Culture, or Catholi-
cism versus Atheism, or the Upper Classes versus the Lower,
or Order versus Anarchy—however one's mind worked.

In a poll of British writers, however, only five avowed they
were for the Nationalists; sixteen were neutral and a hundred
in favor of the Loyalists. The majority of Englishmen weighed
and found the balance in favor of the Republic, and yet Great
Britain formulated and followed a policy of rigid nonintervention
that in reality favored the Nationalists, pressuring France to follow suit. Discretion prevailed over conviction. At the moment,
that was the English way.

and Russia

Even America, the isolated, found itself embroiled. The
Hearst press, the *American Mercury, Time* magazine and Father
Coughlin lined up in the early weeks as loyal Franco partisans.
The Scripps-Howard papers, the *New York Times* and four other
New York dailies were said to have pro-Loyalist sympathies.
Catholic Al Smith was pro-Franco; Catholic Westbrook Pegler
was anti.

Secretary of State Cordell Hull, Ambassadors Joseph P. Ken-
nedy and William C. Bullitt urged nonintervention. Cabinet members Henry Morgenthau, Jr., and Harold Ickes and the President's wife, Eleanor, urged aid to the Republicans.

Two brigades, the Lincoln and the Washington, composed of
Americans, were organized to fight in Spain on the Loyalist side.
But an embargo was enacted by Congress which more than threw
the balance in favor of the Nationalists.

Even the names used to designate the belligerents added to
the confusion: Nationalists, Insurgents; Reds or Communists;
Spanish Government Forces or Loyalists; Rebels; Mutineers;
Anarchists; Socialists; Revolutionaries; Monarchists; Royalists;
anti-Fascists; leftists; Fascists; Falangists; Traditionalists — without first pausing to think, it was difficult to remember which
applied to whom.

And what of Spain itself? The ideological issues were so heady and so confused, so filmed-over, eventually, by a membrane of treachery, violence and guilt, that all suffering and nobility seemed compromised.

George Orwell, the British novelist, who went to enlist in the Loyalist army, wrote:

> I knew there was a war on, but I had no notion what kind of a war. If you had asked me why I had joined the militia I should have answered: "To fight against Fascism," and if you had asked me what I was fighting *for,* I should have answered: "Common Decency." I had accepted the . . . version of the war as the defence of civilization against a maniacal outbreak by an army of Colonel Blimps in the pay of Hitler.

After some months in the field he returned to Barcelona to observe, "What the devil was happening, who was fighting whom and who was winning, was at first very difficult to discover."

"In this war there are many foolish things," Hemingway made one of his Republican soldiers say in *For Whom the Bell Tolls.* "In this war there is an idiocy without bounds." Things might seem crystal clear to hotheaded partisans outside of Spain, but inside it was murky in the extreme.

> In fact, it would be hard to find an atmosphere more full of envy, intrigues, rumor, and muddle than that which exists at the moment in the capitals of Republican Spain [wrote pro-Loyalist British writer, Cyril Connolly]. The farther one gets from the front, the dimmer grows the memory of the 19th of July, the louder the mutual accusations and reproaches of the parties . . . it seems useless to clamour for unity of command when there is no one worthy of it.

Intellectuals like Ortéga y Gasset and Menéndez Pidal fled the Republic in despair after endorsing its cause. The great humanist, Miguel de Unamuno, Rector of the University of Salamanca, who initially had supported the Nationalist movement as

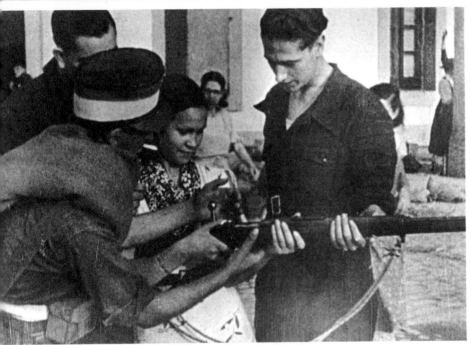

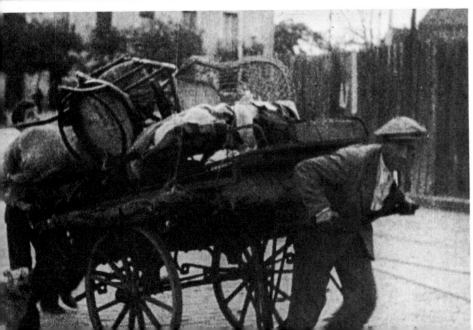

a "struggle for civilization against tyranny," turned against the Insurgents under the most embarrassing and dramatic conditions. At an august University ceremony, honored by the presence of Señora Franco and Nationalist hero General Millán Astray, Unamuno suddenly could bear no more. Addressing his remarks to the magnificently maimed general (an eye, arm, leg and half his remaining fingers had been shot away) he denounced him as a "cripple who lacks spiritual greatness. . . . You will win, because you possess more than enough brute force, but you will not convince, because to convince means to persuade. And in order to persuade you would need what you lack — reason and right in the struggle. I consider it futile to exhort you to think of Spain. I have finished."

He had indeed. A few days later in his quarters, where he had been kept under house arrest, he died of a cerebral hemorrhage — or a broken heart.

If the ideological issues were hopelessly confused and agonizing, what of the fighting, the actual pattern of attack and counterattack, of campaigns, advances and retreats?

DEEP IN THE WINTER PLAIN, TWO ARMIES
DIG THEIR MACHINERY, TO DESTROY EACH OTHER.
MEN FREEZE AND HUNGER. NO ONE IS GIVEN LEAVE
ON EITHER SIDE, EXCEPT THE DEAD AND WOUNDED,
THESE HAVE THEIR LEAVE; WHILE NEW BATTALIONS WAIT
ON TIME AT LAST TO BRING THEM VIOLENT PEACE.

Thus wrote Stephen Spender.
Orwell, too, has left a few vivid memories:

. . . the winter cold, the ragged uniforms of militiamen, the oval Spanish faces, the Morse-like tapping of machine-guns,

Actors in a Spanish Tragedy

the smells of urine and rotting bread, the tinny taste of bean-stews wolfed hurriedly out of unclean pannikins.

The whole period stays by me with curious vividness. In my memory I live over incidents that might seem too petty to be worth recalling. I am in the dugout at Monte Pocero again, on the ledge of limestone that serves as a bed, and young Ramón is snoring with his nose flattened between my shoulder-blades. I am stumbling up the mucky trench, through the mist that swirls round me like cold steam. I am halfway up a crack in the mountain-side, struggling to keep my balance and to tug a root of wild rosemary out of the ground. High overhead some meaningless bullets are singing.

I am lying hidden among small fir-trees on the low ground west of Monte Oscuro, with Kopp and Bob Edwards and three Spaniards. Up the naked grey hill to the right of us a string of Fascists are climbing like ants. Close in front a bugle-call rings out from the Fascist lines. Kopp catches my eye and with a schoolboy gesture, thumbs his nose at the sound. . . .

I am walking up and down the line of sentries, under the dark boughs of the poplars. In the flooded ditch outside the rats are paddling about, making as much noise as otters. As the yellow dawn comes up behind us, the Andalusian sentry, muffled in his cloak, begins singing. Across no man's land, a hundred or two hundred yards away, you can hear the Fascist sentry also singing.

Beyond the incongruous juxtaposition of violence and beauty, of hostility and atonement that many sensitive men have discovered in battle, Orwell found that the war had a disquieting triangular quality; that although the Franco forces were only mildly distracted by their dependence on German and Italian aid and by the differences between the Monarchists and the Falange, the Loyalists were hopelessly compromised, demoralized, corrupted by their dependence on Russia — that the Communists, Socialists, Anarchists, Democrats that made up their camp continually threatened them with a war within a war.

On both sides the war was poor in heroes that one could name by name.

For the Loyalists there was El Campesino, the Communist general nicknamed "the Peasant." "With his black beard, his thick negroid lips, and his feverish, staring eyes," Hemingway wrote, "he was a brave, tough man; no braver in the world. But God, how he talked too much . . ."

Of Lister, a quarryman trained in Russia to become a Communist general, Hemingway said: "He was a true fanatic and he had the complete Spanish lack of respect for life. In few armies since the Tartar's first invasion of the West were men executed summarily for as little reason as they were under his command." The Anarchist Durruti was ruthless and intelligent, and undependable. The woodcutter Juan Modesto was likewise Russian-trained and a committed Communist. Miaja, the "Saviour of Madrid," was "Old, bald, spectacled, conceited, stupid-as-an-owl, unintelligent-in-conversation, brave-and-dumb-as-a-bull, propaganda-built-up . . ."

> There wasn't any Grant, nor any Sherman nor any Stonewall Jackson on either side [Hemingway concluded]. No, nor any Jeb Stuart either. Nor any Sheridan. It was overrun with McClellans though. The Fascists had plenty of McClellans and we had at least three of them.

On the Fascist side only the dead and Franco seemed free to retain their heroic attributes. Three of the principal rivals for the supreme power, should the Nationalists win, disappeared in the course of the war. José Antonio Primo de Rivera Saenz de Heredia, the founder of the Fascist Falange Española, was martyred by the Republicans at the Alicante prison. General Mola Vidal and General Sanjurjo Sacanell, "the Lion of the Rif," both conveniently died in airplane crashes.

Calvo Sotelo disappeared before the war began. He "was a very good Fascist, a true Spanish Fascist," one Hemingway character said. "Franco and these other people are not. . . . He was

very intelligent and it was very intelligent that he was killed. . . ."

Although the pro-Loyalists could make out a case for optimism almost to the very end of the war, the maps and the unadorned listing of the fall of Spanish cities told another and sadder story.

Within a month of the uprising half of Spain was in Nationalist hands. From then on, the catalogue was unrelievedly grim:

Irún fell to the Nationalists on September 4, 1936; San Sebastián on the twelfth. The Nationalist garrison imprisoned in Toledo's Alcázar was relieved by Franco in September. By October, Madrid was under fire. On November 6, the Republican government fled to Valencia, the President to Barcelona. In February Malaga fell.

There were a few respites: the arrival of the International Brigades to relieve Madrid, the Italians' ignominious retreat at Guadalajara.

Then Guernica. The first systematic aerial bombardment of an open town in history saw a population of 7000 reduced by 1654 killed, 889 wounded. At first it seemed merely senseless, excessive brutality. Later it was revealed as a clinical experiment: German bombardiers perfecting their techniques for civilian destruction. There was an international outcry. Picasso had the subject for his most famous work of art. And the dreary catalogue of defeats proceeded as spring of 1937 came.

June 10, Bilbao fell; July 26, the Nationalists recaptured Brunete.

By the end of the first year of war, July 1937, Franco held 35 out of 50 of the country's provincial capitals.

In August, the Nationalists captured Santander, and the Pope recognized Franco's government. In October, Gijón was captured. The Loyalists had lost the North.

*In the twentieth century,
the unarmed too are targets*

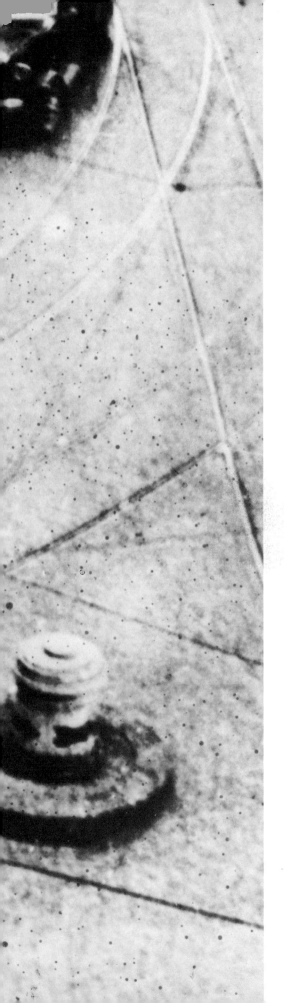

Majorca was now occupied. The Republican government moved from Valencia to Barcelona.

The Loyalists won Teruel in January, held it till the end of February and lost it back. It was their first and last successful offensive.

By the end of March 1938 Catalonia was separated from the rest of Republican Spain and things settled down to a stalemate that showed no indication of breaking. Then came Munich. The democracies abandoned the Czechs to the Axis and in the bargain Spain's fate also was sealed. The International Brigades were withdrawn.

"You can go proudly. You are history. You are legend," La Pasionara told them as they departed. "You are the heroic example of Democracy's solidarity and universality. We shall not forget you, and when the olive tree of peace puts forth its leaves again, mingled with the laurels of the Spanish Republic's victory — come back!"

At the moment, her overlords in Moscow were preparing the way for the German-Russian pact and the end of the democratic solidarity and universality she memorialized.

By December 1938, the Nationalists, bolstered by additional German aid, had launched a devastating new offensive. In January Barcelona fell, and shortly thereafter all Catalonia. The government moved to the French border, then back to Madrid. In February, Britain and France recognized Franco as the legal head of the Spanish Government. The surrender of Madrid on March 29 ended it all.

LIFTING UP OUR HEART TO GOD, WE GIVE SINCERE THANKS WITH YOUR EXCELLENCY FOR SPAIN'S CATHOLIC VICTORY

Pope Pius wired Generalissimo Franco. The date was March 31, 1939. The world's attention was already occupied elsewhere.

Victory embrace: Franco and comrades-at-arms

On March 16, 1939, the Nazis had taken over Bohemia and Moravia. On March 31, Prime Minister Neville Chamberlain, finally tried beyond his monumental patience, declared that Britain and France "would lend the Polish Government all support in their power" should Poland also be attacked.

"I'll cook them a stew they'll choke on!" the Fuehrer shouted in a rage when he heard the news.

The rehearsal was over. The principal players were preparing to take their places.

THE LAST DAYS

ON AUGUST 23, 1939, German Foreign Minister Joachim von Ribbentrop and Vyacheslav M. Molotov, a new Russian Commissar for Foreign Affairs especially appointed for the occasion, met in Moscow and signed the ten-year Russo-German Nonagression Pact. The irreconcilable extremes, the diametrical opposites, the supposed poles of the Years Between had willingly coalesced. This act of supreme cynicism brought the era that had begun with Versailles to an end. An epoch, which had briefly flirted with the millennium, and then uneasily embraced the squalid and expedient present, shuddered and collapsed.

In just one week what everyone expected and dreaded, yearned for and abhorred, took place. What the betrayals of Italy and Germany and Spain had left unilluminated suddenly became so patently clear that the most ridiculously self-deceiving could not avoid the lesson. Evil is one, even when it is at war with itself. God is not mocked.

Eleven months previous, the pride of free Europe had had its final humiliation at Munich when Prime Minister Chamberlain of Great Britain and Premier Daladier of France had delivered up to Hitler and his henchmen a large part of the sovereign state of Czechoslovakia.

Ignoring pledges implied and explicit, France and Great Britain acquiesced to Czchoslovakia's being stripped of 11,000 square miles and 3,600,000 people, 66 per cent of her coal and 80 per cent of her lignite, 70 per cent of her iron and steel, 80 per cent of her cement and textiles, 40 per cent of her timber, 70 per cent of her electrical power supplies, and 86 per cent of her glass and chemicals. Poland and Hungary took generous helpings; and on March 16 of the new year, some thirteen days before the fall of Madrid, Hitler, occupying Prague, proclaimed the end of the Czechoslovakian Republic with no one to gainsay him.

Now, less than six months later, the golden apple had already spent its force. Hitler was mounting his last deception.

The pact — a deadly fantasy, concocted in a spirit of total and mutual hypocrisy — stated that for the next ten years the old and predictable antagonists, Russia and Germany, would be bosom pals; that they would consult each other regarding common interests and adjust by peaceful means any conflicts which might arise between them. Nor would they join "any grouping of powers that is directly or indirectly aimed at the other party."

Off to Moscow

With a gasp of horror, that figment of the liberal imagination, collective security, now vanished. Those who had since the October Revolution tried honestly to equate Russian terrorism with anti-fascism and the idealism of the future finally had to admit failure. Those even more benighted, who had seen in Hitler a legitimate bulwark against Bolshevism, were confounded. And affixed to the publicly announced treaty was a secret protocol. In it Hitler, the apotheosis of the political Right, and Stalin, the apogee of the Left, agreed to the apportionment of those sections of Europe lying between them.

"The Nonaggression Pact and Consultation Pact which Molotov and I signed yesterday evening is a firm and unshakable foundation on which both states will build and come into close co-operation. This is perhaps one of the most significant turning-points in the history of two peoples." Prescience and cant blended in Ribbentrop's official announcement in Moscow.

Stalin proposed a toast: "I know how much the German nation loves its Fuehrer. I should therefore like to drink to his health."

First dibs was Germany's; and her choice was Poland.

The sides lined up: England and France avowed to defend Poland against outside invasion. Italy was bound to Germany by the "Pact of Steel." Russia was pledged to neutrality. This time, both sides sensed the bluff would be called. The final ten days of the double decade began to flick away.

Molotov and Ribbentrop: The opposites meet

August 23:

In London, the day the pact was announced, crowds stood in Downing Street from dawn watching diplomats and ministers enter and leave Number 10, as though in the inscrutable faces under the hard hats they could read the common future. All English reservists were alerted, and London windows ordered darkened. An embargo was put on the exporting of essential war materials and a sizable segment of the British Fleet steamed into the Skagerrak between the Norwegian and Danish coasts.

Paris, deserted as usual in August, witnessed a steady stream of uniformed men heading toward the German frontier. At Cherbourg 1200 Americans sailed for home aboard the German liner *Bremen;* from Le Havre, on the French liner *Normandie,* 1400 more departed — including screen favorites Sonja Henie, George Raft, and Constance Bennett.

The same day, in Brussels, the foreign ministers of seven small countries — Norway, Sweden, Finland, Denmark, the Netherlands, Luxembourg and Belgium — called for peace.

King Leopold observed: "Our continent seems about to commit suicide in a frightful war, out of which can come neither victors nor vanquished, but which will engulf the spiritual and material values created by centuries of civilization. Let the conscience of the world reawaken . . . a durable peace can be founded only on a moral order. . . . Hundreds of millions of men are one with us in the heartfelt hope of halting the race to war."

The building of fortifications in Poland went on, day and night.

August 24:

German bombers filled the sky over Berlin, and its colonies of foreigners were growing thin. In Warsaw, the radio was broadcasting that *Poland will fight even if she has to go it alone,* and private cars and taxis were being requisitioned. Polish families began to store up food, matches, alcohol stoves.

President Roosevelt, just back from a vacation in New Brunswick and Newfoundland, already pledged to a policy of preserving "peace with honor," sent appeals to Hitler, President Ignacy Mościcki of Poland and King Victor Emmanuel of Italy. The State Department advised 59,000 Americans abroad to return home.

In London, in the House of Commons, Prime Minister Chamberlain, the architect of Munich, announced the end of "appeasement": "If, despite all our efforts to find a way of peace — and God knows I have done my best—if, in spite of all that, we find

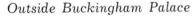

At Number 10 Downing Street

Outside Buckingham Palace

Toward Poland

ourselves forced to embark upon a struggle which is bound to be fraught with suffering and misery for all mankind, and the end of which no man can foresee; if that should happen, we shall not be fighting for a political future of a far-away city in a foreign land. We shall be fighting for the preservation of those principles of which I have spoken and the destruction of which would involve the destruction of all possibilities of peace and security for the peace of the world."

In Paris, the City of Light, weak bulbs were being substituted for strong in the street lamps, to prevent their being seen from the air.

At Castel Gondolfo, in Fascist Italy, Pope Pius XII appealed for peace in an address which was afterwards read in English, French, German and Polish:

"Justice advances with strength of reason, not with arms. Empires that are not founded on justice are not blessed by God. Dangers are imminent, but there is still time. Nothing is lost by peace; everything may be lost by war. . . ."

That same day, passenger ships in Italian ports were forbidden to leave. Mussolini met with his chiefs of staff to tally up what his price for coming in with Hitler should be.

August 25:

On the afternoon of August 25, Hitler explained to Britain's Ambassador to Germany, Nevile Henderson, his German alliance with Russia. In contrast to the last war, Germany would no longer have to fight on two fronts, he explained. The agreements would also render Germany secure economically for the longest possible period of war. In the afternoon, the Italian Ambassador gave Hitler's pact Mussolini's servile blessing, and promised that Italy would support Germany in Poland politically and economically. Military support, he added, would depend on Germany's delivering supplies and raw materials to resist predictable British and French attacks. Then followed a bill of particulars for a twelve-month war.

Truckloads of soldiers in full field equipment drove through the Brandenburg Gate and down Unter den Linden.

Berlin

In Warsaw air-raid trenches were dug in all parks and public squares, and householders were equipped with gas masks.

In Washington, President Roosevelt said it was his personal opinion that war was far from certain, and that he was optimistic that a peaceful solution could be found. Nevertheless, that afternoon the State Department announced that plans for the evacuation of Americans from Europe had been made, and the Italian liner *Roma* canceled a West Indies cruise.

In London, the English and Poles formalized their Agreement of Mutual Assistance. Hospital patients were moved to the country to make way for possible air-raid casualties. Buildings were sandbagged, and air-raid shelters dug; the National Gallery was closed and the Coronation Chair in Westminster Abbey was packed for transport to a safe place. J. P. Morgan handed over his shooting box in Scotland for use as a wartime hospital.

In Paris, Premier Daladier spoke grimly:

". . . With the life and liberty of Poland . . . the destiny of other European peoples is linked. Our destiny and that of every other French citizen is involved. There is not one of you who does not understand that, if by lack of foresight or by cowardice we permit all these peoples to succumb one after another . . . after having broken our word, betrayed our ideal and misunderstood our vital interests, we shall find ourselves without friends and without support, and that very soon this effort to dominate Europe will turn quickly against our own country . . ."

Daladier had also prepared a message for Hitler: "There is nothing today which need prevent any longer the pacific solution of the international crisis with honour and dignity for all peoples, if the will for peace exists equally on all sides."

In the meantime French engineers cut the pontoon bridges across the Rhine, and all permanent railroad bridges leading into Germany were mined.

"Der Fuehrer has ordered the mobilization, without public proclamation, of the bulk of the Wehrmacht," the Chief of Hitler's High Command directed.

London

August 26:

Huge red posters appeared in the Berlin railroad stations reading, *Beginning August 27, travelers will no longer have the right to transportation.* French Ambassador Coulondre called on Hitler to deliver Daladier's plea for peace, and urged its message, talking to Der Fuehrer for forty minutes. "Perhaps I moved him," Coulondre reported, "but I did not prevail. His stand was taken."

Along the Franco-German border, opposite the Maginot Line, Germans were busy constructing pillboxes every one hundred yards.

In London, the Jewel House in the Tower of London and the State Apartments at Windsor were closed and their treasures removed to safety. The stained glass in Canterbury Cathedral was buried somewhere in the surrounding countryside, and a plan for killing all dangerous animals in the London Zoo was announced.

Churchill, returning from France, told a newspaper reporter that he thought it was "too late for appeasement" and that "Poland probably will be attacked shortly and a historic error of one hundred and fifty years ago will be repeated." Later he was to comment on what he observed that day: "It is a curious fact about the British Islanders, who hate drill and have not been invaded for nearly a thousand years, that as danger comes nearer and grows, they become progressively less nervous; when it is imminent, they are fierce; when it is mortal, they are fearless. These habits have led them into some very narrow escapes."

In Paris, the Louvre was closed, and at Chartres the stained glass windows were taken from their tracery.

The mobilization: Britain; France; Poland; Germany

NEXT PAGE: *The Siegfried Line; The Maginot Line*

Into Danzig

August 27:

Hitler replied to Daladier's plea for peace with the words:

"Since yesterday the situation has become still more acute. . . . I must warn you that we shall strike at the first incident. . . . I would fight with my people for the reparation of an injustice, while the others would fight for its retention."

The justice Hitler demanded included the free city of Danzig, the Polish Corridor, and everything that Germany lost in 1918, including Posen and Silesia.

Food rationing was announced, to begin the following day.

In Warsaw, while thousands watched an international soccer match between Poland and Hungary, volunteers — including the city's mayor — dug more trenches. All food shipments to Danzig from Poland were halted.

In Britain, details of London weather were omitted from the weather report, and the United States ship *President Roosevelt* left Southampton for New York with 4,125,000 pounds of

he Polish cavalry

gold on board, bringing to twenty million pounds the shipments of the past three days.

In Paris, the crowds attending church noticeably increased, with some worshipers carrying gas masks. A sudden rash of bouquets appeared on the tomb of France's Unknown Soldier under the Arc de Triomphe.

In Strasbourg, a jeering crowd gathered outside the German travel bureau and, although both sides of the Rhine were blacked out, a brilliant moon illuminated every detail of the freshly poured machine-gun turrets and barbed wire.

August 28:

The whole of Berlin — in vans, grocery trucks, army lorries — seemed to be moving east. Sir Nevile Henderson arrived at the Reich's Chancellery wearing a red carnation, supposedly his emblem of optimism. He had an hour in Hitler's presence, during which, he reported later, the Fuehrer seemed friendly.

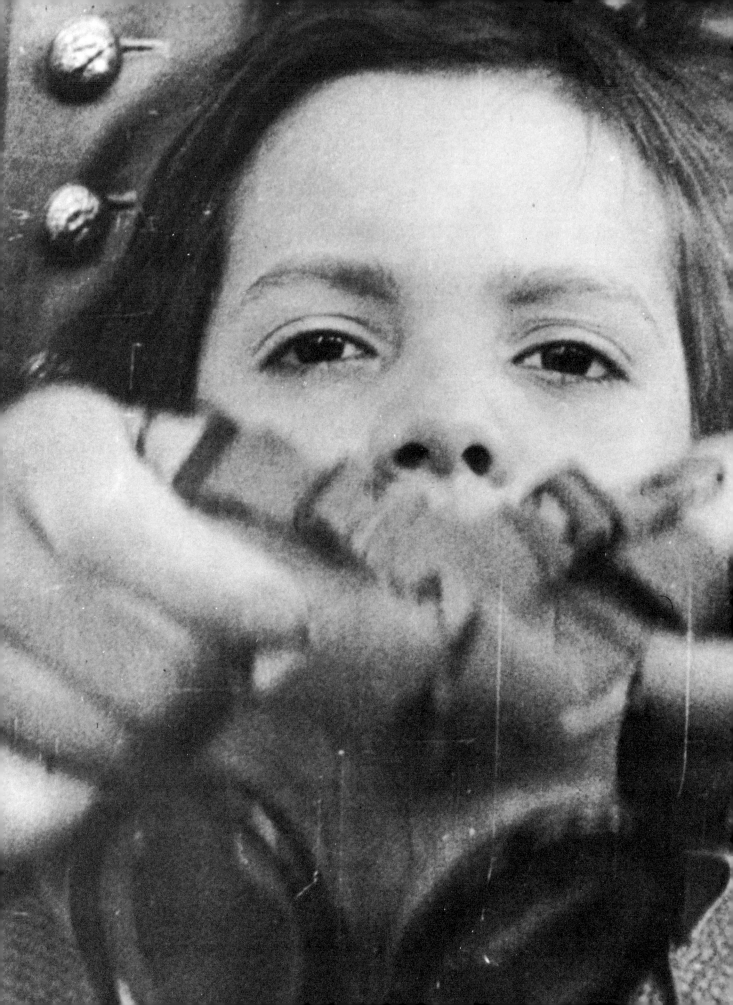

In New York, Pan-American painted American flags on planes flying to Europe, to avoid "misunderstandings." The *Bremen* and the *Normandie* both docked.

In London the traffic lights were hooded and the city was suffused with the smell of wet paint as curbs and trees were zebra-striped to help motorists during black-out. British vessels were banned from the Mediterranean, and 650,000 London schoolchildren, bearing rations and gas masks, trooped back to school.

The French-German border was closed and the Dutch, the Belgian and the Swiss governments ordered army mobilization.

August 29:

Hitler, somewhat less friendly, issued an ultimatum to British Ambassador Henderson, demanding that Poland dispatch to Berlin an emissary with full powers to receive and answer German proposals, and that he arrive not later than midnight of August 30, 1939. Parenthetically he revealed that his army and air force were ready to strike, and had been since August 25.

Henderson reported to Lord Halifax that "the only result can be either war, or once again victory for him by a display of force and consequent encouragement to pursue the same course again next year or the year after." Eleven months after Munich, the German troops completed their occupation of Slovakia.

In the United States, the German liner *Bremen* was searched for contraband, and military guards were ordered stationed on all ships passing through the Panama Canal. In Louisiana, a retired naval commander put forward five thousand dollars and a plan to buy the Polish corridor and Danzig for Hitler.

In Russia, troops were massing along the Polish border.

In London, the social columns of the *Times* were full of announcements of weddings updated "owing to the crisis," and the guards at Buckingham Palace were provided with bombproof shelters next to their sentry boxes.

The stained glass windows of the Cathedral of Strasbourg were removed.

King Leopold of Belgium and Queen Wilhelmina of the Netherlands offered their good offices to Great Britain, France, Germany, Italy and Poland.

August 30:

From Warsaw, British Ambassador Sir Howard Kennard reported: "I feel sure that it would be impossible to induce the Polish Government to send . . . any . . . representative immediately to Berlin to discuss a settlement on the basis proposed by Herr Hitler. They would certainly sooner fight and perish rather than submit to such humiliation."

In Berlin, von Ribbentrop told Ambassador Henderson it would be unthinkable and intolerable for him to invite the Polish Ambassador to a meeting to discuss German demands.

J. P. Morgan and a record number of passengers left Southampton aboard the *Queen Mary,* and gas masks were furnished to the Vatican guards.

August 31:

Berlin restaurants began using paper napkins to conserve soap, and the Polish Ambassador spent the morning on the phone to Warsaw, his last communication before the lines were cut. Henderson, after a two-hour meeting with Goering, informed the British Government that it would be useless for him to make any further suggestions.

Great Britain mobilized her navy to full strength and called up her army and air force reserves. In Paris any building showing a light had its electricity cut off, and in Italy Mussolini invited the great powers to a conference within a week.

In Moscow the Supreme Soviet unanimously ratified the Russo-German Nonaggression Pact, and Molotov proclaimed:

"This pact not only eliminates the menace of war with Germany, it narrows the zone of possible hostilities in Europe and serves thereby the cause of universal peace; it must open to us new possibilities for increasing our strength for further consolidation of our position, for a further growth of the influence of the Soviet Union on international developments."

At 5:11 A.M., September 1, 1939, Hitler issued a proclamation to the German army, and at 5:45 A.M. Germany launched her attack across the Polish frontier.

Hitler's words were: "The Polish State had refused the peaceful settlement of relations which I desired, and had appealed to arms. Germans in Poland are persecuted with bloody terror and driven from their houses. A series of violations of the frontier, intolerable to a great Power, prove that Poland is no longer willing to respect the frontier of the Reich. In order to put an end to this lunacy, I have no other choice than to meet force with force from now on. The German army will fight the battle for the honor and vital rights of reborn Germany with hard determination. . . . Long live our people and our Reich!"

To the Reichstag later, and by radio to the world at large, he announced: "This night for the first time Polish regular soldiers fired on our own territory. Since 5:45 A.M., we have been returning the fire, and from now on bombs will be met with bombs. I will continue this struggle, no matter against whom, until the safety of the Reich and its rights are secured. My whole life henceforth belongs more than ever to my people. I am from now on just first soldier of the German Reich. I have once more put on that coat that was the most sacred and dear to me. I will not take it off again until victory is secured, or I will not survive the outcome."

"There will come, sometime in the vengeful providence of God," Woodrow Wilson had told the good people of Sioux City, Iowa, just twenty years before, *"another struggle in which not a few hundred thousand fine men from America will have to die, but as many millions as are necessary to accomplish the final freedom of the peoples of the world."*

The vengeful providence of Wilson's God had expressed itself. The world once more had a cynosure and a challenge. The Years Between were at an end.

SOURCES

1: EVANGEL OF PEACE; PROPHET OF DOOM

William Bolitho: *Twelve Against the Gods—The Story of Adventure*. New York: Simon and Schuster, Inc. Copyright 1929 by Simon and Schuster, Inc. Renewed 1957 by Cybil Bolitho Fearnley.

Herbert Hoover: *The Ordeal of Woodrow Wilson*. New York, Toronto, London: McGraw-Hill Book Company, Inc. Copyright 1958 by Herbert Hoover.

2: ACROSS THE RIVER AND INTO THE HILLS

George Antheil: *Bad Boy of Music*. Garden City, N.Y.: Doubleday, Doran and Company, Inc. 1945.

Sylvia Beach: *Shakespeare and Company*. New York: Harcourt, Brace and Company. Copyright 1956, 1959 by Sylvia Beach.

Diana Cooper: *The Light of Common Day*. Boston: Houghton Mifflin Company. 1959.

Malcolm Cowley: *Exile's Return—A Literary Odyssey of the 1920's*. New York: Viking Press. Copyright 1934, 1937, 1945, 1951 by Malcolm Cowley.

Margaret Crosland: *Colette—A Provincial in Paris*. New York: British Book Centre, Inc. Copyright 1954 British Book Centre, Inc.

Cecil B. De Mille: *Autobiography*. Ed. Donald Hayne. New York: Prentice Hall. 1959.

Scott Fitzgerald: *The Crack-Up*. New York: New Directions. Copyright 1931 Charles Scribner's Sons; Copyright 1933 by Editorial Publications; Copyright 1934 and 1936 by Esquire, Inc.; Copyright 1935 by F-R Publishing Corporation; Copyright 1945 by New Directions.

Scott Fitzgerald: *The Last Tycoon*. New York: Charles Scribner's Sons. Copyright 1941 by Charles Scribner's Sons.

Douglas Goldring: *The Last Pre-Raphaelite—The Life of Ford Madox Ford*. London: MacDonald and Company, Ltd. 1948.

Ben Hecht: *A Child of the Century*. New York: Simon and Schuster, Inc. Copyright 1954 by Ben Hecht.

Phil A. Koury: *Yes, Mr. De Mille*. New York: G. P. Putnam's Sons. 1959.

Charles A. Lindbergh: *"We."* With a foreword by Myron T. Herrick. New York-London: G. P. Putnam's Sons. Copyright 1927 by Charles A. Lindbergh.

Elsa Maxwell: *R.S.V.P.—Elsa Maxwell's Own Story*. Boston and Toronto: Little, Brown and Company. Copyright 1954 by Elsa Maxwell.

Arthur Mizener: *The Far Side of Paradise—A Biography of F. Scott Fitzgerald*. Boston: Houghton Mifflin Company. Copyright 1949, 1950, 1951 by Arthur Mizener.

Lloyd Morris: *Not So Long Ago*. New York: Random House, Inc. 1949.

Grant Overton, ed.: *Mirrors of the Year: A National Review of the Outstanding Figures, Trends, and Events of 1926–1927*. New York: Frederick A. Stokes Co. Copyright 1927 by Frederick A. Stokes Co.

Albert Bigelow Paine: *Life and Lillian Gish*. New York: The Macmillan Company. Copyright 1932 by The Macmillan Company.

D. D. Paige, ed.: *The Letters of Ezra Pound, 1907–1941*. New York: Harcourt, Brace and Company. Copyright 1950 by Harcourt, Brace and Company, Inc.

Leo Rosten: *Hollywood: the Movie Colony*. New York: Harcourt, Brace and Company. 1945.

Frank Scully: *Rogue's Gallery: Profiles of My Eminent Contemporaries*. Hollywood: Murray and Gee, Inc. Copyright 1943 by Frank Scully.

Gertrude Stein: *Autobiography of Alice B. Toklas*. New York. Harcourt, Brace and Company. Copyright 1933 by Harcourt, Brace and Company, Inc.

Gertrude Stein: *Portraits and Prayers*. New York: Random House, Inc. Copyright 1934 by Random House, Inc.

Gertrude Stein: *Everybody's Autobiography*. New York: Random House, Inc. Copyright 1937 by Random House, Inc.

Nathanael West: *The Day of the Locust*. New York: Random House, Inc. Copyright 1939 by the estate of Nathanael West.

Edmund Wilson: *The Shores of Light—A Literary Chronicle of the Twenties and Thirties*. New York: Farrar, Straus and Young, Inc. Copyright 1952 by Edmund Wilson.

3: IL DUCE AND BAPU

Tommaso Antongini: *D'Annunzio*. Boston: Little, Brown and Company. 1938.

Louis Fischer: *The Life of Mahatma Gandhi*. New York: Harper and Brothers. Copyright 1950 by Louis Fischer.

Homer A. Jack, ed.: *The Wit and Wisdom of Gandhi*. With introduction by Homer A. Jack. Boston: Beacon Press. 1951.

Margherita Sarfatti: *The Life of Benito Mussolini*. Translated from the Italian by F. Whyte. London: Butterworth and Company, Ltd. and New York: Frederick A. Stokes. 1925.

Vincent Sheean: *Lead Kindly Light*. New York: Random House, Inc. Copyright 1949 by Vincent Sheean.

Madeleine Slade: *The Spirit's Pilgrimage*. New York: Coward-McCann. Copyright 1960 by Madeleine Slade.

Dennis Mack Smith: *Italy*. Ann Arbor: The University of Michigan Press. Copyright 1959 by the University of Michigan.

Frances Winwar: *Wingless Victory*—A biography of Gabriele D'Annunzio and Eleanora Duse. New York: Harper and Brothers. Copyright 1956 by Frances Winwar.

4: A VIOLENT FLOWERING

Sheldon Cheney: *The Story of Modern Art*. New York: The Viking Press. Copyright 1941 by Sheldon Cheney.

William Kahn: *Einstein—A Pictorial Biography*. New York: The Citadel Press. Copyright The Citadel Press, 1955.

Leo Lania: *Today We Are Brothers*. Boston: Houghton Mifflin Company. 1942.

William L. Shirer: *Berlin Diary—The Journal of a Foreign Correspondent, 1934–1941*. New York: Alfred A. Knopf, Inc. Copyright 1940, 1941 by William L. Shirer.

William L. Shirer: *The Rise and Fall of the Third Reich.* New York: Simon and Schuster, Inc. Copyright by William L. Shirer, 1959, 1960.

Nicolas Slonimsky: *Music Since 1900.* New York: W. W. Norton Company. 1938. Copyright 1953 by Coleman-Ross Company, Inc.

Ernst Toller: *Seven Plays.* New York: Liveright Publishing Corporation. 1936.

5: WAILING DAY ON WALL STREET

The Autobiography of Will Rogers. Selected and edited by Donald Day. Foreword by Bill and Jim Rogers. Boston: Houghton Mifflin Company. Copyrights by the Curtis Publishing Company and the Rogers Company. 1949.

John Kenneth Galbraith: *The Great Crash, 1929.* Boston: Houghton Mifflin Company, 1954. Copyright 1954, 1955 by John Kenneth Galbraith.

6. THE VOICES

Gordon W. Prange, ed.: *Hitler's Words.* Introduction by Friederich Schuman. Washington: American Council on Public Affairs. 1944.

Franklin D. Roosevelt: *On Our Way.* New York: The John Day Company. Copyright 1934 by Franklin D. Roosevelt.

Franklin D. Roosevelt: *Nothing to Fear: The Selected Addresses of Franklin Delano Roosevelt 1932–1945,* with an introduction and historical notes by B. D. Zevin. Boston: Houghton Mifflin Company. Copyright 1946 by Houghton Mifflin Company.

Arthur Schlesinger Jr.: *The Coming of the New Deal.* Boston: Houghton Mifflin Company. Copyright by Arthur Schlesinger Jr. 1958.

Edmund Wilson: *The American Earthquake—A Documentary of the Twenties and Thirties.* Garden City, N.Y.: Doubleday and Company, Inc., Doubleday Anchor Books. Copyright 1958 by Edmund Wilson.

7: THE PALL

John Steinbeck: *The Grapes of Wrath.* New York: The Viking Press. Copyright 1939 by John Steinbeck.

8: THE BRAVE AND THE FAIR

Hector Bolitho: *King Edward VIII.* Philadelphia, London: J. B. Lippincott Company. Copyright 1937 by Hector Bolitho.

Iles Brody: *Gone with the Windsors.* Philadelphia: Winston. 1953.

Thelma, Lady Furness, and Gloria Vanderbilt: *Double Exposure—A Twin Autobiography.* New York: David McKay Company. Copyright 1958 Gloria Morgan Vanderbilt and Thelma, Lady Furness.

Will Rogers: *The Autobiography of Will Rogers.* Selected and edited by Donald Day. Foreword by Bill and Jim Rogers. Boston: Houghton Mifflin Company. Copyrights by the Curtis Publishing Company and the Rogers Company 1949.

Windsor, Duchess of: *The Heart Has Its Reasons—The Memoirs of the Duchess of Windsor.* New York: David McKay Company. Copyright 1956 by the Duchess of Windsor.

9: THE LITMUS WAR

Cyril Connolly: *The Unquiet Grave*. New York: Harper and Brothers. 1945.

Cyril Connolly, ed.: *The Golden Horizon*. With an introduction by Cyril Connolly. New York: British Book Centre. 1953.

Robert Graves and Alan Hodge: *The Long Week End*. New York: The Macmillan Company. Copyright 1941 by The Macmillan Company.

Ernest Hemingway: *For Whom the Bell Tolls*. New York: Charles Scribner's. Copyright 1940 by Ernest Hemingway.

Koestler, Arthur and Others: *The God That Failed*. Edited by Richard Grossman. New York: Harper and Brothers. 1949.

George Orwell: *Homage to Catalonia*. Harcourt, Brace and Company. Copyright 1952 by Sonia Brownell Orwell.

Hugh Thomas: *The Spanish Civil War*. New York: Harper and Brothers. Copyright 1960 by Hugh Thomas.

PICTURE SOURCES

book design by Betty Binns